POLICY STUDIES IN EMPLOYMENT AND WELFARE NUMBER 20

General Editor: Sar A. Levitan

Indian Giving
Federal Programs for
Native Americans

Sar A. Levitan and
William B. Johnston

The Johns Hopkins University Press, Baltimore and London

This study was prepared under a grant from The Ford Foundation.

The Johns Hopkins University Press, Baltimore, Maryland 21218
The Johns Hopkins University Press Ltd., London

Library of Congress Catalog Card Number 75-11354

ISBN 0-8018-1739-0 (cloth)
ISBN 0-8018-1740-4 (paper)

Library of Congress Cataloging in Publication data will be found on the last printed page of this book.

Contents

v

CONTENTS

List of Tables

List of Charts

Preface

The growing national awareness of minority rights has belatedly reached native Americans, and, at long last, the federal government is reappraising its posture toward, and its programs for, Indians. There is dawning recognition that native Americans must be freed from federal dominance, no matter how well intentioned, and that Indian tribes and individuals must have more control over the development of their lives and institutions.

This process will be painfully slow. Years of federal mismanagement and inattention have built up an inertia that can only be changed gradually. Much rhetoric has been expended to speed this change, but realities impose obstacles because there is disagreement among various groups of Indians, federal agencies, and Congress as to what and how changes should occur. Most critically, two centuries of federal support and control have left Indians ill-equipped financially or politically to take over complete responsibility for their reservations. Inevitably, the process of evolving self-determination will be long and difficult.

This watershed in federal policy toward native Americans is

an appropriate time to assess both the socioeconomic status of Indians and their relationship to the federal government. A complete survey of demographic, social, and political aspects would take many hundreds of pages and require detailed analysis of the differing conditions among different tribes. The aim of this volume is more modest: to sketch the highlights of conditions on reservations, to outline the scope of federal aid, and to suggest the nature of the problems and choices that lie ahead. Little sound, factual information is available concerning native Americans, and this book seeks partially to fill this gap.

We are indebted to Siobhan Oppenheimer Nicolau, of the Ford Foundation, Robert Crane, of the Native American Economic Development Corporation, and officials of the Bureau of Indian Affairs, Public Health Service, and Office of Education for critical and helpful reviews of the manuscript.

This study was prepared under a grant from the Ford Foundation. In accordance with the Foundation's practice, complete responsibility for the preparation of the volume was left to the authors.

January 1975   Sar A. Levitan
William B. Johnston
Center for Manpower Policy Studies
The George Washington University

1

Indian Population

According to the U.S. Bureau of the Census, there were 793,000 people who identified themselves as American Indians living in the United States in 1970, plus 34,000 Eskimos and Aleuts.[1] In 1973, the Bureau of Indian Affairs, which has responsibility only for those living on or near reservations, estimated that 543,000 Indians, Eskimos, and Aleuts in the twenty-five reservation states were eligible for its services. Evidently, a substantial majority of Indians still live close to their reservations, though many are moving away.

Most reservations are in the West, and 77 percent of all Indians live west of the Mississippi. The largest numbers of Indians live in Arizona, New Mexico, Oklahoma, California, and Alaska. Although there are 481 identified tribal entities in the United States, half of all Indians belong to nine tribes (some of which have several subgroups). Their estimated populations in 1970 were:

(thousands)

Navajo	96.7	Cherokee	66.2	Sioux	47.8
Chippewa	41.9	Pueblo	30.9	Lumbee	27.5
Choctaw	23.6	Apache	23.0	Iroquois	21.5

The customs, social and economic conditions, and legal status of these tribes vary so widely that generalizations are hazardous. As a result of different cultural histories and experiences during the nineteenth-century period of white encroachment, the two largest tribes are quite unlike each other. The largest tribe, the Navajo, resides mostly on or near its reservation, maintaining its traditions and, generally, participating little in white society. Median education is 5.3 years; median family income is $3,400. By contrast, few of the second largest tribe, the Cherokee, live on their reservation in North Carolina. With 10.4 median years of school and a median family income of $6,400, the Cherokees are clearly far more assimilated into the social and economic mainstream. It is thus misleading to lump members of these Indian tribes together as though their experiences or characteristics were identical or even very similar.

Most large tribes have their own reservations, though some tribes share lands with others. Altogether, there are over 280 Indian reservations, by far the largest of which is the Navajo, with 22,000 square miles in Arizona, New Mexico, and Utah. Most reservations are much smaller, ranging from the 8,000 Sioux living on 2,600 square miles at Pine Ridge, South Dakota, to many tiny reservations of tens or hundreds of acres, some with no Indians living on them. Indian lands total about 52.6 million acres, or 2.3 percent of the land area of the United States.

Migration

The lure of employment opportunities and official federal policy encouraging migration has drawn increasing numbers of Indians from reservations to the cities since World War II. Between 1960 and 1970, the census count of urban Indians more than doubled, from 165,000 to 340,000. On the other hand, the number living in rural areas grew by only 11 percent, from 380,000 to 423,000,[2] despite a birth rate that added 51 percent to the total Indian population. Although urban-rural figures are not identical with reservation-nonreservation numbers, it is clear that many Indians have left the reservation for the city in the past decade (chart 1). By 1970, several cities had larger Indian populations than any reservation except the Navajo.

(*thousands*)

Los Angeles	23.9
Tulsa	15.2
Oklahoma City	13.0
San Francisco	12.0
Phoenix	10.1
New York City	10.0

Indians off the reservation present a startling contrast to those who remain behind. Urban Indians are far better educated and have much lower unemployment rates, two-thirds greater average family income, fewer dependent children, and half the chance of being in poverty as those on reservations. In fact, by such standards as family income, male labor force participation, percentage of high school graduates, dependents per bread-winner, and poverty status, Indians in metropolitan areas are better off than metropolitan blacks (table 1).

Whether these dramatic differences between on-reservation and off-reservation Indians are the result of greater economic and educational opportunities in urban areas, the product of selective migration of the ablest and best-educated Indians from the reservations, or simply undercounting by the census of transient and poverty-ridden urban Indians, it is clear that the most disadvantaged Indians are those on reservations. Although discrimination still plays a part, particularly in some urban labor markets in the Southwest, isolation is the key barrier to Indian economic progress. Urban Indians (especially those living in small cities and towns near reservations) suffer severe economic and social problems, but their difficulties are not as great as those of reservation Indians. For this reason, and because the federal responsibility for Indians is limited to those on or near reservations, most studies of Indians properly focus on the situation of rural, reservation Indians.

3

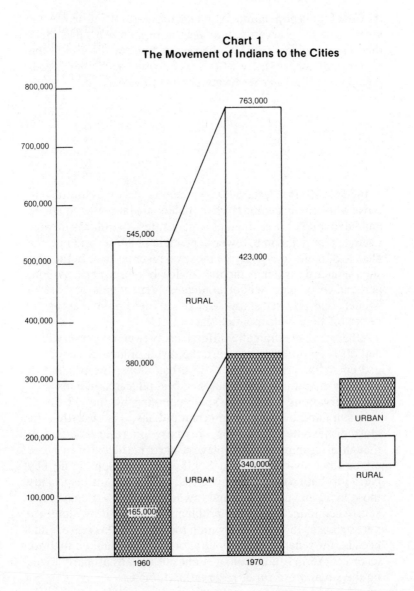

Chart 1
The Movement of Indians to the Cities

Table 1. Characteristics of Indians on Reservations and in Standard Metropolitan Statistical Areas Compared with Other Races, 1970.

	Indians on reservations*	Indians in SMSA	Blacks in SMSA	All Races in SMSA
Median family income	$4,088	$7,566	$6,832	$10,474
Number of children under 18 per family head	3.0	1.8	1.9	1.4
Median years of education (persons over age 25)	7.6	11.5	10.4	12.1
Population in poverty	54.9%	23.3%	28.2%	10.9%
Male labor force participation (age 16 and over)	50.3%	73.0%	72.0%	78.3%
Male unemployment rate (age 16 and over)	18.6%	8.4%	6.3%	3.8%
High school graduates (persons age 25 and over)	21.9%	42.5%	36.7%	55.3%

*Averages for Indians living within the boundaries of the 115 largest
reservations.
SOURCE: U.S. Bureau of the Census, *1970 Census of the Population, American Indians,* PC(2)1F (June 1973), Tables 11-14; idem, *General Economic
and Social Characteristics,* PC(1)C1 (June 1973), Tables 107-29.

Federal Policy and Indian Legal Status

The complex legal and political status of Indians and their
tribes is anomalous to the situation of any other population
subgroup or governmental unit. Initially, Indian tribes were
legally viewed as conquered nations to whom the United States
owed protection under its signed treaties. In 1871, Congress
ended its recognition of Indian tribes as nations empowered to
sign treaties with the United States, although previous treaties
were not nullified. This confused legacy of still enforceable
treaties gives Indian tribal governments greater powers in some

cases than those of the states but places them under complete federal dominance, since the government holds title to the land on which they live, and the courts have held that the federal government has considerable authority over, and responsibility for, Indian affairs. This includes the responsibility to provide educational systems, health services, and welfare and social assistance.

Indian tribes have the right to establish conditions for tribal membership, to choose their form of government, to levy taxes, to regulate domestic relations, to set property law, and to administer justice. In matters coming under tribal jurisdiction, there is no appeal above the legal system on the reservation. Congress, however, has placed some limitations on tribal powers. For example, in at least one case, tribal officials were designated by the BIA, and in other cases federal statutes have extended state criminal jurisdiction onto the reservations. In 1968, the Indian Civil Rights Act limited Indian jurisdiction to crimes punishable by no more than a $500 fine or six months in jail and extended constitutional guarantees to persons charged under tribal judicial systems.

Individually, Indians have the same rights as other U.S. citizens, having been granted citizenship rights in 1924. They are subject to federal laws and must abide by state laws when they are off the reservation. They vote, are subject to the draft, pay taxes, and may hold office. The only major difference in Indian status is in regard to the tribal or individual lands held in trust by the federal government. Neither these lands nor the income derived from them are subject to state and local taxation, and they may not be sold or transferred without the approval of the federal government.

Federal policy toward Indians has zigzagged between the conflicting aims of assimilation and separation. Initially, the policy was to segregate Indians in designated areas, where they were to be "protected" and provided for as wards of the government. Throughout the nation's westward expansion during the early 1800s, federal officials followed a policy of negotiated and forced removal of Indians from eastern areas of white settlement to more remote western areas. The early resettlements were strongly resisted by eastern tribes, and during the 1800s the plains Indians fought bitterly against accepting federal reservations. The final removal of the last Indians onto reservations was not completed until after the massacre of the Sioux at Wounded Knee, South Dakota, in 1890.

Almost as soon as the process of placing the Indians on reservations had been completed, policy shifted to encouraging their assimilation into society at large, which, it was hoped, would allow the eventual termination of special federal programs and trust relations. Indians on reservations were encouraged and sometimes forced to abandon tribal traditions, and an educational system aiming to instill white values was developed. In 1887, the Dawes Act provided for the allotment of plots up to 160 acres of Indian lands to "competent" Indian individuals. It was hoped that these Indian farmers would develop the self-sufficiency to grow out of their dependent federal status. This allotment policy continued for nearly fifty years, despite the fact that it did not have the effects envisioned by its planners, resulting primarily in the loss of three-fifths of all Indian land. In many cases, Indians sold out to whites, lived on the assets until the money was gone and then returned to dependence on federal reservations.

After the issuance of the federally commissioned Meriam Report in 1928, which was sharply critical of Indian policies, Congress passed the Wheeler-Howard Indian Reorganization Act in 1934. This act ended allotment and encouraged the development of Indian reservations and the professionalization of the Bureau of Indian Affairs. It also provided for the improvement of Indian education and the reestablishment of Indian self-government. In the two decades following this act, some progress was made toward these goals. After World War II, however, sentiment again developed for terminating the federal government's special relationship with Indians, culminating in 1953 with the passage of a congressional resolution that declared termination to be the official federal policy. In the next five years, the trust status of a number of tribes was ended, including that of the Menominees in Wisconsin, the Klamaths in Oregon, and several tribes in Oklahoma, Utah, and California.

By the early 1960s, the policy of termination had again been discredited by protests from both Indians, who preferred to remain separate political entities, and others, who argued that Indians were not ready for complete independence. In the last decade the pendulum has returned, and Indian reservations again are to be supported and developed, now, however, under the aegis of Indians themselves. Administrations from Kennedy's to Nixon's have enunciated policies aimed at developing Indian human and natural resources on the reservations, while allowing Indians to control and administer federal assistance programs. Under the banner of self-determination, Indians have been encouraged to develop their tribal resources and governments free from the threat of termination of their special federal status. Since this goal coincided with the Nixon and Ford administration policies of decentralizing federal authority, self-determination has achieved new momentum since 1968, with a growing share of financial and operational responsibility for Indian affairs being turned over to the tribes.

Currently, the federal government spends over a billion dollars a year on programs directed toward Indians. Almost half of this money is channeled through the BIA to support its educational, resource development, and social support programs, and another fifth goes to the Department of Health, Education, and Welfare to fund the Indian Health Service. Many other agencies spend substantial sums on reservation Indians, including the Departments of Agriculture (rural electrification, food stamps). Commerce (economic development loans and assistance), Health, Education, and Welfare (supplementary educational funds, public assistance, community action programs, Head Start), Housing and Urban De-

Table 2. Federal Expenditures for Indians, Fiscal 1973 (in Millions)

Bureau of Indian Affairs		$ 494.4
Education	$187.3	
Welfare and social service	116.3	
Resource management	83.1	
Construction	56.0	
Road construction	45.5	
Administration	6.2	
Department of Health, Education, and Welfare (incl. OEO)		404.3
Public assistance	71.0	
Indian health	198.0	
Education	112.3	
Office of Native American Programs	23.0	
Department of Labor		47.9
Department of Housing and Urban Development		34.8
Department of Commerce		31.1
Department of Agriculture		26.6
Small Business Administration		19.8
Veterans Administration		16.4
Department of Interior, except BIA		9.0
TOTAL		$1,084.3

SOURCE: U.S. Congress, House, *Department of the Interior and Related Agencies Appropriations for 1974, Part 4, Hearings* before a subcommittee of the Committee on Appropriations, 93d Cong., 1st sess. (Washington, D.C.: Government Printing Office, 1973), pp. 562, 569–70; idem, *Department of the Interior and Related Agencies Appropriations for 1975, Part 1, Hearings* before a subcommittee of the Committee on Appropriations, 93d Cong., 2d sess. (Washington, D.C.: Government Printing Office, 1974), p. 160.

velopment (subsidized public housing), and Labor (manpower training) (table 2).

This concentration of federal assistance (approximately $2,000 per reservation Indian) means that the economies and social structures of reservations are totally dominated by the federal presence. The school system, health system, public works, and public services are provided by federal dollars. Nearly half of all jobs held by Indians living within reservation boundaries are government jobs. Three-fifths of all personal income of reservation Indians originates from federal coffers. This dollar dominance obviously complicates efforts to allow Indians self-determination and control of their own lives. Moreover, it indicates that it is impossible to analyze the problems or conditions of reservation Indians independently of the federal programs designed to alleviate these problems. For Indians, far more than for any other group, socioeconomic status is a federal responsibility, and the success or failure of federal programs determines the quality of Indian lives.

2

Economic Conditions and Economic Development

Income and Employment

With the exception of blacks living in rural areas, Indians on reservations have the lowest income of any group in the United States. In 1969 median family income for all rural Indians was barely half that for rural whites (table 3). More than half of rural Indian families received less than $5,000 in 1969, compared to only one-fifth of white families in the same income bracket. Among Indians residing within reservation boundaries, median family income was only $4,088, two-fifths of the white median.

When the effects of large Indian families are added, per capita income comparisons are even more bleak. Even after adjustments for residence, Indian per capita income is only half that of whites. Since more Indians live in rural areas, the overall Indian average is below $1,600 per year, the lowest among any ethnic group. Among Indians on the 115 largest reservations surveyed by the census in 1970, per capita income was only $962, less than a third of the national average for all whites, and only three-fifths of levels for blacks and Chicanos (chart 2). Even this figure disguises the depths of Indian poverty in some areas. For example, on the Papago reservation in Arizona per

Table 3.   Median Family Income of Indians by Residence, 1969

	Total	Urban	Rural, Nonfarm	Rural, Farm
Indian	$5,832	$ 7,323	$4,691	$4,319
Black	6,067	6,581	4,035	3,445
Chicano	6,962	7,256	5,329	5,020
White	9,961	10,629	8,542	7,534

SOURCE: U.S. Bureau of the Census, *1970 Census of the Population, American Indians*, PC(2)1F (June 1973), Table 9; idem, *General Economic and Social Characteristics*, PC(1)C1 (June 1973), Table 94; *Persons of Spanish Origin*, PC(2)1C, (June 1973), Table 10.

capita income in 1969 was $588, and for the Navajo reservation it was $776—levels not far above those in underdeveloped countries (table 4).

During the 1960s, Indian income rose relatively faster than that of whites. The median income for Indian men in 1959 was 35 percent as much as for whites, but 51 percent in 1969. For families the gains were smaller. Comparisons of overall distributions of Indian and white families indicate that Indians had less than 62 percent as much income as whites in 1959, but 66 percent in 1969. All of this small gain came from migration to urban areas, where Indians were relatively better off. Relative Indian family income distribution actually deteriorated compared to whites in both urban and rural areas:

Ratio of Income Overlap Indian/White*

	Total	Urban	Rural
1959	62%	77%	66%
1969	66%	71%	62%

*DERIVED FROM: U.S. Bureau of the Census, *U.S. Summary*, PC(1)1C, Table 95 (1962); idem, *Non-White Population by Race*, PC(2)1C, Table 15 (1963); idem, *U.S. Summary*, PC(1)C1, Table 94 (1972); idem, *1970 Census of the Population, American Indians*, PC(2)1F, Table 9 (1973).

The obvious explanation for this continuing poverty is the lack of employment opportunities on reservations. Most Indian

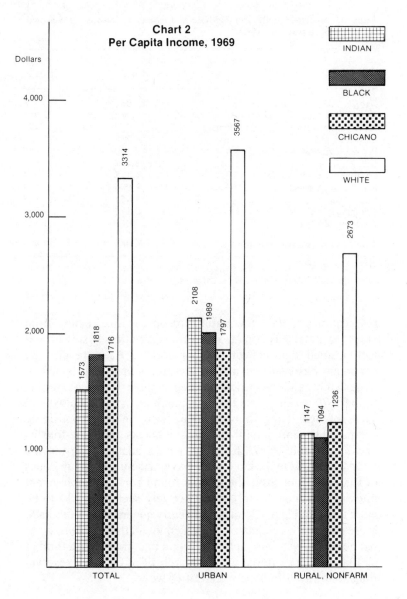

Chart 2
Per Capita Income, 1969

Table 4. Median Family and Per Capita Income of Indians on Selected Reservations, 1969

	Family	Per Capita
Navajo, Arizona	$3,084	$ 776
Pine Ridge, South Dakota	3,912	1,042
Joint Use (Navajo and Hopi), Arizona	2,052	472
Blackfeet, Montana	4,258	1,087
Papago, Arizona	2,500	588
Gila River, Arizona	3,417	813
Cherokee, North Carolina	4,125	1,034
San Carlos, Arizona	4,006	687
Hopi, Arizona	3,454	833
Laguna, New Mexico	6,115	1,345
Flathead, Montana	5,045	1,513
Total, 115 largest reservations	4,088	962

SOURCE: U.S. Bureau of the Census, *1970 Census of the Population, American Indians,* PC(2)1F (June 1973), Table 14.

reservations contain few natural resources, are remote from large markets, have inadequate transportation systems, and lack trained and educated labor forces. As a result, the economic base on and near reservations is usually small or nonexistent, and the critical problem is joblessness. According to the 1970 census, little more than half of Indian men over 16 years of age living in rural areas were in the labor force compared to more than three-fifths of blacks and three-fourths of whites (table 5). With so few jobs available, many of the nonparticipants in the labor force have evidently given up hopes of finding a job. Still, the census found rural unemployment rates (which include only those actively seeking work) to be more than double black rates and nearly quadruple white totals. More recent BIA estimates, which count all those able to work but not working as unemployed, found that more than a third of all Indians were without jobs in March 1973. On some reservations, half of all Indians were out of work.

Table 5. Male Labor Force Participation and Unemployment, 1970

	Number Employed (in Thousands)			Participation Rate (Percentage)			Unemployment Rate (Percentage)		
	Indian	Black	White	Indian	Black	White	Indian	Black	White
Total	117	6,449	43,030	63.4	69.8	77.4	11.6	6.3	3.6
Urban	62	5,220	31,365	72.0	71.9	78.3	9.4	6.6	3.6
Rural	55	1,229	11,665	55.8	61.0	75.8	14.0	5.9	3.7
115 largest reservations	(22)	---	---	(50.3)	---	---	(18.6)	---	---

SOURCE: U.S. Bureau of the Census, *1970 Census of the Population, American Indians,* PC(2)1F (June 1973), Tables 4 and 12; idem, *General Economic and Social Characteristics,* PC(1)C1 (June 1973), Table 90.

Percentage without jobs

Hopi	49
Pine Ridge	39
Blackfeet	37
Navajo	35
Papago	29
Rosebud	22
Cherokee	22
Gila River	18

During the 1960s Indian employment status improved slightly, though comparisons between 1959 and 1969 are clouded by cyclical factors. Overall, the Indian unemployment rate declined by 4.5 percentage points and labor force participation rose by 4 points during the decade. But Indian status relative to whites did not improve, with ratios between black, white, and Indian unemployment varying less than 10 percent.

The jobs that are available in reservation economies reflect the dominant influence of government. Almost half of all jobs on Indian reservations are state, local, and federal positions, delivering the services provided by the BIA, the Health Service, and other agencies. This percentage is three times the national average for government employment. By contrast, employment rates in wholesale and retail trade and in manufacturing are far below proportions common in the rest of the economy (table 6).

In terms of occupational status, Indians are predictably concentrated on the lowest rungs. Surprisingly, however, the occupational status of Indian men is considerably better than that of blacks, with higher proportions of professionals, managers, salesworkers, and craftsmen, and with fewer operatives, laborers, and service workers (table 7). Another important but little noticed aspect of reservation economies deserves attention: the limited and declining importance of agriculture and forestry. Though Indian lands constitute the chief natural resource on reservations, farming and forestry employ only one-tenth of Indian men. Since 1940, the decline in farm employment among Indian men has been dramatic (chart 3). Though these figures are for all Indians, even on reservations

Table 6. Distribution of Employed Indians by Industry, 1970

	(Percentage) Indians on Reservations	Urban Indians	All Races, United States
Total	100.0	100.0	100.0
Agriculture, forestry, and fisheries	10.2	2.4	3.7
Construction	8.4	7.2	6.0
Manufacturing	15.5	24.4	25.9
Transportation, communications, and other utilities	4.7	6.3	6.7
Wholesale and retail trade	7.8	17.3	20.0
Personal services	5.6	7.6	4.6
Professional services	25.4	18.3	17.6
Other, including public administration, business, and repair services	22.4	16.6	15.2
(Government workers)	(46.0)	(19.3)	(16.1)

SOURCE: U.S. Bureau of the Census, *1970 Census of the Population, American Indians,* PC(2)1F (June 1973), Tables 4, 7, 12, and 13; idem, *General Economic and Social Characteristics,* PC(1)C1 (June 1973), Tables 80 and 92.

Table 7. Occupational Distribution of Indian Males, 1970

	(Percentage) Indian Total	Urban	Rural	Black	White
Professional and technical	9.2	11.4	6.8	5.7	14.9
Managers and administrators	5.0	5.8	4.2	2.8	12.4
Sales	2.4	3.2	1.5	2.0	7.3
Clerical	5.7	7.3	3.9	8.0	7.5
Crafts	22.1	23.1	20.9	15.4	21.9
Operatives	23.9	25.6	22.1	29.5	18.8
Laborers	13.2	10.8	15.8	16.1	6.0
Farmers and managers	2.3	0.2	4.6	0.9	2.8
Farm laborers	5.7	1.8	10.2	3.6	1.5
Service workers	10.4	10.8	10.1	15.9	7.3

SOURCE: U.S. Bureau of the Census, *1970 Census of the Population, American Indians,* PC(2)1F, (June 1973), Table 7; idem, *Occupational Characteristics,* PC(2)7A (June 1973), Table 2.

17

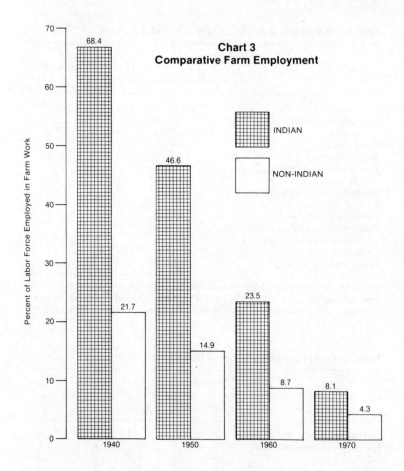

Chart 3
Comparative Farm Employment

only 12 percent of Indians were employed in farm occupations by 1970.

The economic picture that emerges from these facts is one of unrelieved blight. With limited natural resources and few incentives for business development, the economic base of most reservation areas consists of government expenditures for social welfare. The educational, health, social, and economic services provided by the government employ the largest segment of the labor force. Transfer payments support another sizable group. Despite the impact of so many government dollars, 55 percent of all Indians on reservations live in poverty.

In addition to social welfare programs (discussed later), federal efforts to improve economic conditions on reservations fall into two main categories: (1) developing agricultural, forest, and mineral resources and (2) establishing and subsidizing industrial and commercial enterprises. Support is also provided for the social overhead investments necessary to business establishment, such as sewer, water, and road systems. Finally, for those for whom no jobs are readily available, direct employment opportunities are subsidized. Altogether, various federal agencies spent $186 million on economic development projects on Indian lands in fiscal 1973 (table 8). Besides outlays by the BIA for resource development programs, the largest expenditures were made by the Economic Development Administration and the Small Business Administration, which provided funds for industrial development.

Agricultural, Forest, and Mineral Resource Development

Indian lands make up the greatest part of personal and tribal Indian wealth. Of approximately 55 million acres reserved for Indian use, almost 40 million are tribally owned, more than 10 million are held by Indian individuals, and 5 million are owned by the government. The primary land use is grazing, with relatively small acreages suitable for irrigated farming, mineral recovery, or timber production.

	(percentage)
Open grazing	61
Noncommercial timber (grazing)	16
Commercial timber	10
Oil and gas	6
Dry farming	3
Other minerals	2
Irrigated farming	1
Other	1

Table 8. Federal Expenditures for Resource Management and Economic Development on Indian Reservations, Fiscal 1973 (in Millions)

Department of Agriculture		$ 11.1
Farmers Home Administration	$ 1.8	
Research Service	1.0	
Stabilization and Conservation Service	3.2	
Rural Electrification Administration	4.5	
Soil Conservation Service	.6	
Department of Commerce		31.1
Business loans	4.9	
Planning and technical assistance	4.2	
Regional action planning	.3	
Economic Development Administration	18.5	
Pribilof Islands Fund	3.2	
Department of the Interior		10.7
Bureau of Sport Fisheries and Wildlife	1.5	
Bureau of Reclamation	7.9	
Geological Survey	1.3	
Bureau of Indian Affairs		113.1
Resource development	51.2	
Construction of irrigation systems	16.8	
Road construction	45.1	
Small Business Administration		19.8
TOTAL		$185.8

SOURCE: U.S. Congress, House, *Department of the Interior and Related Agencies Appropriations for 1974, Part 4, Hearings* before a subcommittee of the Committee on Appropriations, 93d Cong., 1st sess. (Washington, D.C.: Government Printing Office, 1973), pp. 563–64.

Despite the low productivity of range land, the large acreage makes the total value of the production from grazing lands greater than that of any other land use. Cattle and sheep worth about $78 million were raised on Indian lands in 1972, while timber cut from Indian lands had a value of about $38 million. Mineral leases and royalties yielded Indians about $49 million. In terms of net income to Indians, mineral leases, which were pure profit, had greater returns than timber or grazing, which had substantial overheads. Though these land-based returns have been rising (particularly during recent periods of commodity price hikes), they are still fractions of the potential yields that could be realized, because most Indian lands are underutilized and poorly cared for. BIA estimates indicate that farm production could be increased by a third if soil conservation was widely practiced, and that the income from timber, mineral, and surface leases could be nearly doubled through aggressive development and careful management.

Agriculture   Three general categories of farming and ranching occupy most Indians. Grazing, which is the least intensive land usage, takes place on nearly 45 million acres of open and forest land; dry farming is practiced on 1.6 million acres, and 600,000 acres are irrigated. Unfortunately, Indians reap small proportions of the returns from farming. Not only are larger proportions of more productive acreage leased to whites (three-fifths of irrigated lands and three-fourths of dry farmland compared to only one-fifth of range land), but the returns per acre are smaller on Indian-operated farms (chart 4).

In addition to poorer land quality, there are several reasons for lower productivity on Indian farms. One problem is that Indian management of farms tends to be inefficient. Poor planning and negligent care cut Indian crop and livestock yields, in part because of inadequate education and technical assistance, but also in part because most tribes do not have agricultural traditions and have not adapted readily to them. Examples recorded by BIA land operations officers include postponing harvests during ceremonials, failing to ensure high calf yields from cattle herds, and preference for cattle over sheep despite the better adaptability of sheep to many arid areas.[1]

Besides these problems of management, most Indians lack sufficient capital to make the investments in machinery, feed, fertilizer, and buildings that are necessary for high productivity in agriculture. Although the BIA operates a revolving farm loan fund, the level of funding is completely inadequate. About $12 million was available in 1973 for all types of industrial, commercial, and agricultural loans, while needs for agriculture alone were estimated at more than $89 million.[2]

Also, many Indian landholdings are too small to be efficient.

21

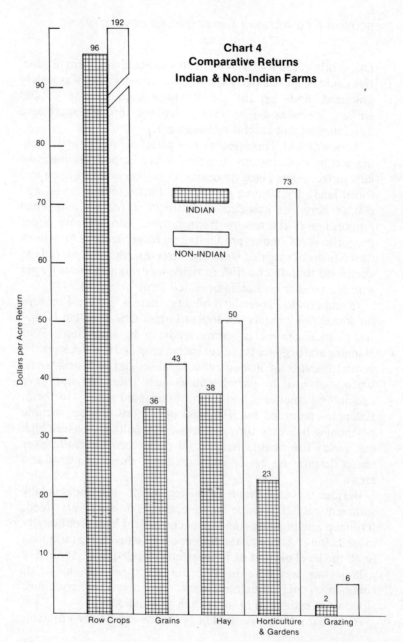

**Chart 4
Comparative Returns
Indian & Non-Indian Farms**

Dollars per Acre Return

INDIAN

NON-INDIAN

| Row Crops | Grains | Hay | Horticulture & Gardens | Grazing |

22

The chief obstacle to reallocating land in tracts of proper size is that landownership has become quite fractionated over the years owing to the cumulative effects of the 1887 Allotment Act. This law provided that the federal government must hold land in trust for all heirs of deceased landowners, rather than assigning it to one person or subdividing it. As a result, only two-fifths of allotted Indian lands have only one owner, and 17 percent have eleven or more. In some cases, where heirs cannot agree on land use, the land may be taken entirely out of production.

Federal efforts to improve Indian agricultural productivity run the gamut from technical assistance in soil and water conservation to range management and legal assistance to help consolidate divided landholdings. The most important efforts from the standpoint of future Indian economic independence and agricultural productivity are irrigation projects. With 600,000 acres already irrigated, the BIA estimated that another 400,000 could be profitably supplied with water. In 1973, the BIA spent $1.6 million on maintenance of irrigation systems and $16.8 million for the construction of new facilities—$10.2 million of which was designated for the huge Navajo project in New Mexico. Destined eventually to cost $250 million and to bring water to 110,000 acres now suitable only for dry grazing, the project has been painfully slow in realization. The first scheduled delivery of water was to have been in 1970, but by 1973 only fifteen of the thirty-three miles of canal from the river to the beginning of the irrigation site were complete. The first block of irrigated land is now scheduled to be opened in the spring of 1976. With water the most precious of resources in the Southwest, and the Colorado River already being utilized at, or near, its capacity, non-Indian water users near reservations have effectively opposed development of the reservation irrigation project by pressuring Congress into holding down annual federal appropriations. Only an outcry raised over proposed cutbacks has prevented the pace of construction from being slowed even further.

The conflicting interests involved in the use of irrigation

23

water are illustrated by programs recently initiated by the BIA for water inventory and water rights protection. Although Indian water rights were guaranteed by a Supreme Court decision in 1906, these rights were to be weighed in an overall plan that took into consideration the competing alternative uses. Since most reservations had no developed irrigation projects and no completed plans for water usage, they were consistently slighted in the allocation of water. "Catch-22" prevailed: to be allocated water, the Indians had to have uses for it, but since no water was available, no projects utilizing irrigation water had been developed or planned. As a result of this impasse, the BIA recently began a complete survey of potential Indian water resources and needs, in preparation for legal action to ensure that Indians receive their share of water. Limited budgets, however, have slowed this survey program and completed inventories are several years into the future.

Of the bright spots in the agricultural situation, some tribal enterprises appear to be the most promising. With superior financial resources, more access to federal aid, and larger farms, several of these collective enterprises have done quite well. The modern cotton plantation operated by the Maricopa Indians in southern Arizona and the livestock associations of the San Carlos Apaches and the Haulapi Indians in the same area have generated employment and income for their tribes.

The overall picture, however, is not sanguine. Relegated to the most arid, least productive lands in the West, lacking an agricultural heritage and benefiting minimally from technical, developmental, and financial aid, most Indian farmers have not advanced much beyond subsistence. Despite programs by the BIA, the Bureau of Reclamation, and the Department of Agriculture, Indians today are not much closer to agricultural self-sufficiency than they were a decade ago. The record of past efforts is not encouraging. Year after year BIA specialists at appropriations hearings cite the same proportions of land eroded, underutilized, or poorly maintained. Some agricultural improvement projects initiated with high hopes have ended in

24

failure. On one project near the Colorado River, more than half of the families who were settled on newly developed irrigation lands left the area within ten years.[3]

It would be naïve to return to the optimism of the 1887 Allotment Act, which foresaw the reservations divided into neat checkerboards of 160-acre family farms. The struggle to make the reservations agriculturally productive will take decades of continued federal help, and even then may not produce the hoped-for returns.

Forestry   Commercial forests occupy about 5.5 million acres of Indian land and in 1974 produced an estimated 930 million board feet of lumber valued at nearly $68 million. In addition, this production generated between five thousand and eight thousand lumbering jobs on or near reservations, of which about three thousand were held by Indians.

Indian timber is unequally distributed. Three percent of the BIA Indian population, living on eight reservations along the Pacific Coast, receive four-fifths of all stumpage payments, and only fourteen reservations receive 96 percent of all Indian timber revenue.

Indian forests are managed by the BIA, whose agents execute leases, negotiate contracts, protect forests from pests and fires, set cutting limits, and develop and improve forest land. For these services, the BIA receives an administrative fee of not more than 10 percent of the stumpage revenue, a percentage that covers costs only in the most productive forests. Tribes may contribute to more intensive management of their own forests and are partly reimbursed for their expenses from BIA management appropriations. The BIA does not spend as much per acre on management as the Forest Service, and it has been criticized for failing to ensure maximum timber harvests. Since the government bears most of the management costs while the Indians reap most benefits, most tribes are eager to have federal forestry investments increased. Such increases, however, are not always warranted, since management costs in less productive forests often exceed total stumpage revenue. Moreover,

25

improvements in forest management may be expected to bring only marginal increases in tribal income. Although reforestation, fertilization, pruning, and thinning might raise yields in a few areas, overall productivity is limited by rainfall and other natural factors.

Besides ensuring that maximum timber, consistent with sustained yields, is harvested annually, the chief potential for development of forest resources lies in the establishment of Indian-owned and-operated forest products industries in areas where timber stands are sufficient. Although there were more than two dozen lumber and wood products factories on or near Indian reservations in 1972, these were located primarily near the less productive Indian forests in the Southwest and Midwest. On reservations in the Pacific Northwest, where the greatest forest resources are located, most timber is sold on the stump, despite the fact that these forests are large enough to support independent lumber companies. Not only do Indians lose the potential profits from milling and processing lumber, but they also miss out on the wages that would be more likely to go to Indians if the mills and plants were owned and operated by the tribes. Indian reservations in general have so few truly valuable natural resources that it is difficult to rationalize why these forest resources—well suited for development by and for Indians—have not been exploited.

Mining   In recent years, most of the income from mineral leases has come from oil and gas leases, with much smaller revenues accruing from coal, asbestos, phosphate, uranium, vanadium, and copper mines. A few Indian tribes have reaped spectacular returns from the discovery of oil on reservation land. In the 1920s, the Osage Indians in Oklahoma received an annual income of about $40,000 per person from oil royalties. More recently, the 178 members of the Tlingit tribe in Alaska have received offers in the millions for their oil-bearing lands. These examples, however, are few and far between, and very few Indians receive much income from mineral resources. Like timber, minerals are unevenly distributed. In 1969, nine reservations received 85 percent of the royalties from oil and gas, and two tribes, the Navajos and the Osage, received about half of all royalties.

Indians generally receive equitable fees for the minerals that have been developed on their lands, though long-term coal contracts signed by some tribes prior to recent energy shortages yield royalties well below the current market price. Besides the oil and gas wells, few other mineral resources produce substantial revenues, though the huge open-pit coal mine on the Navajo reservation and a new copper mine located on the San Xavier reservation in Arizona are exceptions. Recent energy shortages, however, have stepped up exploration for fossil fuels, and the BIA has proposed a comprehensive survey of Indian mineral resources.

Industrial Development

Because of the unequal distribution and limited potential of agricultural and natural resources, federal efforts to develop reservation economies have concentrated during the past fifteen years on enlarging the industrial base of reservations. This program involves not only encouraging businesses to locate on reservations but also creating conditions under which they will survive and prosper. On most reservations the infrastructure necessary to business growth is entirely lacking: road and other transportation systems, public sewer and water facilities, ready sources of electric power or other energy, a trained and centrally located labor force, and banking or other services needed by business. Besides seeking to develop these resources, federal agencies have extended credit and in some cases have negotiated guaranteed contracts with companies planning to locate on the reservation. In fiscal 1974, more than $110 million was spent for these efforts. The largest portions of this sum came from the BIA to build and maintain roads, and from the Economic Development Administration to construct facilities for industrial parks (table 9).

Credit Sources   The initial requirement for new business

27

Table 9. Federal Expenditures for Resource Development, Fiscal 1974 (in Millions)

Bureau of Indian Affairs		$ 57.4
Business enterprise incentives (including		
OJT subsidies)	$ 5.5	
Credit	2.3*	
Road maintenance	6.6	
Road construction	43.0	
Department of Commerce		33.4
Small Business Administration		19.8
TOTAL		$110.6

*Does not include loans extended from BIA revolving funds.
SOURCE: U.S. Congress, House, *Department of the Interior and Related Agencies Appropriations for 1975, Part I, Hearings* before a subcommittee of the Committee on Appropriations, 93d Cong., 2d sess. (Washington, D.C.: Government Printing Office, 1974), pp. 160, 240.

formation is money. Although major companies locating on Indian reservations may be expected to have their own capital, small new companies, particularly those of Indian tribes or individuals, may have few sources of financing. To help fill this gap, the BIA, the Small Business Administration, and the Commerce Department make credit available to new companies establishing plants on or near reservations. New loans extended from the BIA revolving funds amounted to approximately $12 million in fiscal 1974. In addition, the program helped to arrange 23,000 private loans totaling about $24 million (mostly small consumer loans), and 1,500 loans worth $38 million from other federal agencies (primarily from the Commerce Department and the SBA). These loan sources, however, were inadequate compared to estimated needs. In the same year, the BIA computed loan needs for economic development and small business establishment at more than $320 million, several times the aggregate available from all public and private sources.

In November 1973, several Indian leaders established an American-Indian bank with headquarters in Washington, D.C. The Bureau of Indian Affairs, the Economic Development Administration, and the Office of Minority Business Enterprise provided $500,000 for operating funds, and the Office of Economic Opportunity gave an additional grant of $363,000. Originally capitalized for $1 million, the bank hoped to supply Indian credit and banking needs by selling stock to, and taking deposits from, Indian tribes and individuals.

A second initiative to open up the flow of funds to reservations was the passage in 1974 of the Indian Financing Act. This act added $50 million to the revolving loan funds for Indians; provided for federal guarantees, insurance, and subsidies of loans to Indians by private lenders; and established a business development program of grants and technical assistance for Indian-owned businesses. The designers of the new law anticipated that these funds and guarantees would generate up to $200 million in new investments on Indian reservations.

Public Works and Road Construction   Money to start new businesses is of little use without the social overhead that can support businesses. This overhead is mostly lacking on rural reservations. Not a single city on a reservation has as many as 5,000 inhabitants, and only a handful have as many as half that. With so few people, these reservation towns usually lack even the most rudimentary public services, other than electricity.

To make these locations attractive to business, the federal government has invested in both public utility systems and roads to link the isolated communities with outside markets and the surrounding labor force. To help develop the infrastructure on or near reservations, the Commerce Department's Economic Development Administration (EDA) has been spending, since 1965, nearly $20 million a year. These funds have been used to create or upgrade water systems, to build sewage and filtration systems, to install power and communication systems, and to establish other utilities needed by business firms. In most cases the EDA has sought to concentrate its grants for utility development to create industrial parks where industries, labor, and transportation systems can be centralized for greater efficiency. From 1967 to 1972, the EDA spent more than $13 million to build thirty-two industrial parks on twenty-nine reservations. Unfortunately, not all of these projects have been immediately utilized. In 1974, occupancy in the parks averaged about 6–8 percent, and thus the average cost per job created was very high. Critics have placed the blame on the lack of coordination between EDA grants and the efforts of other agencies to attract business. But in some cases it appears that there was an insufficient base for resource development.

The continuing effort by BIA to improve reservation roads is also instrumental in the effort to attract business. The increasing expenditures devoted to this effort are important not only because roads and highways are the Indians' only link with the outside world (few reservations have air or rail connections) but also because these projects employ substantial numbers of Indians and provide opportunities for Indian-owned construction companies. Provided primarily by the BIA, expenditures for road construction and maintenance in fiscal 1974 amounted to $50 million, which was used to pave about 600 miles of road, in addition to providing grading, drainage, bridges, and gravel surfaces for several thousand additional miles. These projects employed considerable numbers of Indians (up to 60 percent of some projects) and supported eleven Indian-owned construction companies.

Still, Indian roads are far from adequate. Eighty-four percent of approximately 22,000 miles of roads maintained by the BIA are dirt surface (nationally, 25 percent of all rural roads are unpaved). Compared to surrounding areas, Indian reservations have many fewer miles of paved road. For example, the Navajo reservation has about 56 miles of all-weather roads per 1,000 square miles, compared with an average of about 150 miles for the surrounding areas of New Mexico and Arizona.

Business Establishment   Despite these recent efforts to improve the attractiveness of Indian lands for new plant locations, reservations are still probably the least hospitable locations for business establishments in the United States. But during the past fifteen years, a combination of technical assistance and feasibility studies, on-the-job training subsidies,

30

guaranteed contracts, credit assistance, and old-fashioned arm-twisting has partly been able to overcome these formidable obstacles and bring new businesses onto reservations. Before 1961, there were only six companies established in Indian labor force areas. By December 1972, there were 230 plants operating on or near reservations employing 7,460 Indians, with an annual payroll of more than $30 million (table 10).

The difficulties of transporting large or heavy products have limited most of these enterprises to small manufacturing operations, typically producing electronic assemblies, wood products, or toys. Most plants employ relatively few workers, the largest (until its closing in 1975) was the Fairchild Industries plant on the Navajo reservation in Shiprock, New Mexico. In 1972, nearly 800 Indians were employed at this facility, producing solid-state electronic components. Excluding this factory, the average number of Indian employees was only twenty-nine per plant. One reason for this small size is that most reservations have relatively small and widely dispersed labor forces.

Table 10. Total Plants in Operation on or Near Reservations

Year	Business Units	Total Indian Employment
1953–60	6	525
1961	8	NA
1962	15	NA
1963	24	NA
1964	40	NA
1965	53	NA
1966	69	NA
1967	89	NA
1968	113	NA
1969	143	NA
1970	169	NA
1971	202	NA
1972	230	7,460

SOURCE: Bureau of Indian Affairs, "Employment in Commercial and Industrial Enterprises Established in Indian Labor Force Areas," December 1972 (mimeo.).

Besides low labor costs, the inducements to these businesses to locate on reservations have varied. The BIA has sought to encourage firms to locate on reservations by providing prospective firms with feasibility assessments and technical advice. In addition, it is common for land leases to be donated and for buildings to be built by tribal authorities to industry specifications. To teach untrained workers required skills and to cut the costs to employers of training new workers, the BIA has subsidized on-the-job training costs of up to one-half the minimum wage (recently raised to 50 percent of the prevailing wage) for workers in the new plants. In 1974, more than 2,000 workers were supported in this manner at an average cost of approximately $1,000 per worker. In some cases, a contract has been negotiated in advance to ensure a market for a new factory's product. For example, in Devil's Lake, North Dakota, the military approved a $125 million order for camouflage nets to be produced at a new plant before construction was begun.

The road to Indian industrial development, however, has not been as smooth as the steadily increasing numbers of plants and workers might indicate. One problem has been the limited degree of Indian investment in and ownership of new plants. The services and small businesses near reservations, such as automobile dealerships, restaurants, liquor and food stores, are still almost exclusively white-owned. And of the newer large plants, many are owned by non-Indian companies (United Mobil Homes, Simpson Electric, and Langer Jewel Bearing). In addition, some tribes have been reluctant to push reservation development aggressively, fearing that it will be followed by termination of reservation status.

Another criticism has been the lack of employment opportunities for skilled male workers at the new plants. Most of the new facilities employ only semi-skilled laborers, and many hire mostly women. This creates resentment in situations where women are hired even though local men cannot find jobs. Another problem has been the lack of industrial discipline among Indian workers. Turnover and absenteeism have been reported to be high and productivity low at some plants, particularly during the early months of operations. Short-sighted workers sometimes quit factory jobs for seasonal jobs paying higher wages for a few weeks. In some cases, personnel problems have been severe enough to force plants to close or to cut back the proportion of Indians in their work forces.[4]

Overall, it is difficult to be very optimistic about industrial development on reservations, despite the rising numbers of new factories during the last few years. The obstacles to profitability are great, and despite the commitment of considerable federal and private resources, attrition is high. Of businesses which opened between 1965 and 1968, at least a third had closed by 1974. Despite the growing numbers, businesses established on reservations employed less than 5 percent of the Indian labor force in 1972. Plans for further development on Indian reservations suffered an agonizing setback in 1975, when Fairchild Camera and Instrument Corporation announced it would not reopen its semiconductor plant in Shiprock, N.M., following an eight-day takeover of the plant by Indian militants. The failure of the Shiprock plant, the largest and best-known reservation enterprise, was sure to slow new development efforts as other companies reappraised their plans in the light of more uncertain business conditions. Though heavier investment, relaxed credit, and other federal subsidies may help underwrite further expansion of business on reservations, the overwhelming drawbacks of these locations make it doubtful that this development effort will reach a self-sustaining stage at any time in the forseeable future.

3

Education

Attainment

Measured by years of school completed and standardized for area, Indians are slightly better educated than other American minorities, but still less schooled than whites. School attainment averages about a year more for Indians than for blacks in similar areas and about three years more than for Chicanos, even though it is from one to three years less than for whites (chart 5). Thirty-three percent of Indians over age twenty-five have graduated from high school, compared to 55 percent of whites and 31 percent of blacks.

The burden of poor education is carried disproportionately by older Indians and by those in rural areas near reservations. Young Indians in urban areas average more than twelve years of school, while those over sixty-five years old on reservations have, on the average, less than grade school preparation (table 11).

The educational attainment of all Indians has been rising steadily during the last two decades, but these gains have not narrowed the overall Indian-white gap. Since 1950 the proportion of Indian males with less than five years of school has

34

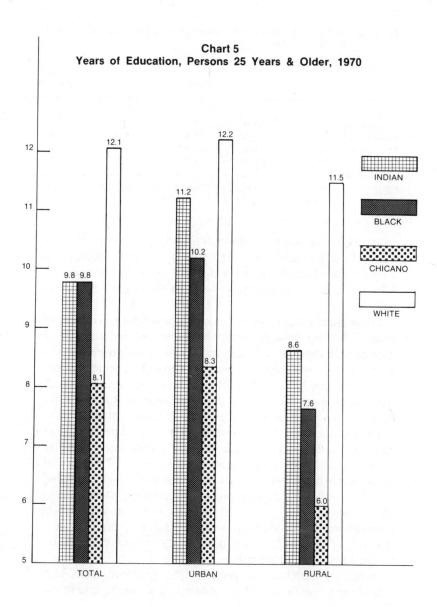

Chart 5
Years of Education, Persons 25 Years & Older, 1970

Table 11. Median Years of School Completed by Indian Males by Age and Residence, 1970

Ages	Total	Urban	Rural, Nonfarm	Rural, Farm
20 to 24 years	12.2	12.4	11.7	11.8
25 to 34 years	11.9	12.2	10.8	10.1
35 to 44 years	10.1	11.4	8.9	8.6
45 to 64 years	8.8	10.3	8.2	8.1
65 years and over	6.6	7.9	5.7	6.2

SOURCE: U.S. Bureau of the Census, *1970 Census of the Population, American Indians,* PC(2)1F (June 1973, Table 5.

fallen from one-third to one-eighth, while the proportion of high school graduates has increased by exactly the reverse proportions. Overall, Indian males have added an average of 2.7 years to their schooling, while white males have added 3.1 years.

These gains reflect the higher ratios of school enrollment of Indian children brought about by increased federal school funding over the past two decades. By 1970, the proportions in school of Indian children of ages five through seventeen years were only slightly lower than the ratios for all races. For ages eighteen to twenty-four years, however, Indians still were only three-fourths as likely as whites to be in school (table 12).

The slightly lower proportions of Indians in school in the late teen years, however, translates into considerably smaller proportions of high school graduates. In 1970, 57 percent of Indian males aged twenty to twenty-four years had graduated from high school, a smaller proportion than the 63 percent of blacks and far below the 85 percent rate for whites. On reservations the dropout rate was even more severe, with less than half of rural Indian men aged twenty to twenty-four years having finished high school.

Increasing numbers of Indians who graduate from high school are going on to college. According to the Bureau of the

Table 12. Educational Enrollment by Age and Residence, 1970 *(Percentage)*

Ages	Total		Urban		Rural, Nonfarm		Rural, Farm	
	Indian	*All Races*	*Indian*	*All Races*	*Indian*	*All Races*	*Indian*	*All Races*
5 and 6 years	69.7	72.4	72.0	76.1	68.9	63.3	63.0	61.4
7 to 13 years	95.1	97.3	95.9	97.6	94.6	96.4	94.9	96.9
14 to 17 years	86.8	92.7	86.3	93.3	86.7	90.7	90.6	92.8
18 to 24 years	23.2	32.2	24.4	34.5	21.5	23.3	27.1	27.7

SOURCE: U.S. Bureau of the Census, *1970 Census of the Population, American Indians*, PC(2)1F (June 1973), Table 3; idem, *General Economic and Social Characteristics*, PC(1)C1 (June 1973), Table 73.

Census, 14,200 Indians were enrolled in college in March 1970, 2,000 more than the total number of Indian college graduates. A survey of colleges by the federal Office for Civil Rights in the fall of 1970 produced even more encouraging results.[1] According to the school administrators (who may have had an incentive to inflate the totals since the schools were under pressure from the Office for Civil Rights to raise their minority enrollment ratios), 28,500 American Indians were on their rolls, including 60 medical and dental students, 190 law students, and 1,300 other postgraduates. Based on the census figures, approximately 12 percent of Indians of ages eighteen to twenty-four years were in college in 1970, compared with 15 percent of blacks and 27 percent of whites.

The evidence indicates that, once in college, Indians are about as likely to stay on until graduation as other students. Among students receiving BIA college scholarship grants (which includes most Indian college students), the dropout rate was about 48 percent, compared with a national average of about 47 percent who left school before graduation.[2]

Educational Performance

In addition to the educational deficits among Indians in years of school and lesser likelihood of enrollment, Indian students perform more poorly in school than whites. In the 1966 Survey of Educational Opportunities, James Coleman found that in contrast to blacks and Spanish-speaking minorities, Indian children start school with relatively small aptitude disadvantages compared with whites: 0.1 of a standard deviation on nonverbal tests and 0.5 for verbal tests. But Indians, like other disadvantaged minorities, do not benefit as much from schooling. By the sixth grade, Indian performance on aptitude and achievement tests ranged from 1.7 to 2.0 years behind average white levels, and by the twelfth grade, it had fallen from 3.2 to 3.9 grades back.[3] (These results include larger numbers of urban than rural or reservation Indian school children.)

The Indian School System

In some measure, the responsibility for these disappointing results must be borne by the BIA, which has established and administered schools for Indians since the signing of treaties with the tribes during the nineteenth century. Initially, most federal schools were boarding schools, established in the belief that Indian assimilation could best be accomplished by removing children from the influence of their cultures and their parents. When the dismal educational results and the often oppressive environments of these institutions were exposed in the 1928 Meriam Report, federal policy de-emphasized boarding schools and sought to shift as many children as possible to day schools or to nearby state and local public schools. Because reservation Indians paid no local property taxes to support public schools, however, Congress authorized federal reimbursement for those schools enrolling Indian children under the Johnson-O'Malley Act of 1934. This assistance was later supplemented under other laws with funds for school construction and operation in federally impacted areas. In addition, Indian schools have become eligible for funds under the 1965 Elementary and Secondary Education Act and have benefited from a variety of other special national education programs, including bilingual education, library resources improvement, Head Start, and Follow Through. Finally, in 1972, Congress passed the Indian Education Act, which provided additional funds to local agencies educating Indians and authorized support for special programs for Indians in public schools. Concern over potential duplication from these appropriations has led to recent changes requiring that states choose between the programs under which they receive federal assistance. All told, the multiple federal funding sources provided $430 million for Indian education in fiscal 1974 (table 13).

According to the BIA count, these funds supported a total of 204,000 Indian students in fiscal 1973, of whom 188,000 were between the ages of five and eighteen years. Of these younger

39

Table 13. Federal Aid to Indian Education, Fiscal 1974 (in Millions)

Elementary and Secondary Education		$350.8
Federal facilities (BIA)	$146.5	
Assistance to public schools (BIA)	25.4*	
Head Start (HEW)	13.0	
ESEA and related programs (HEW)	52.5*	
School construction (BIA)	27.0	
Other HEW programs	86.4*	
Adult, Vocational and Higher Education		77.6
Adult education and vocational education (BIA)	21.2	
Adult and vocational education (HEW)	14.6	
Higher education (BIA)	22.8	
Higher education (HEW)	19.0	
TOTAL		$428.4

*Although these funds are appropriated for Indian education, in some cases they are diluted among all children in the eligible school districts.

SOURCE: U.S. Congress, House, *Department of the Interior and Related Agencies Appropriations for 1975, Part I, Hearings* before a subcommittee of the Committee on Appropriations, 93d Cong., 2d sess. (Washington, D.C.: Government Printing Office, 1974), pp. 425–27, 219–28.

students, 69 percent were in public schools, 25 percent were in federal schools, and 6 percent were in other types of schools, mostly missionary. On a cost-per-child basis, federal schools were far more expensive than most public school systems (chart 6). These higher expenditures for BIA schools reflect the greater costs for transportation, staffing, housing, dormitories, and other expenses involved in operating a widely dispersed, multiple-purpose school system for relatively small numbers of students per facility.

The assistance given to public schools enrolling Indians has recently been the focus of the greatest federal attention. Since the passage of the Johnson-O'Malley Act, school districts near reservations have repeatedly claimed that federal supplements are inadequate to cover the costs of educating large numbers of Indian children. A series of laws boosting the federal share for Indian education in public schools has created a system of

Chart 6
Expenditure per Pupil, Fiscal 1973

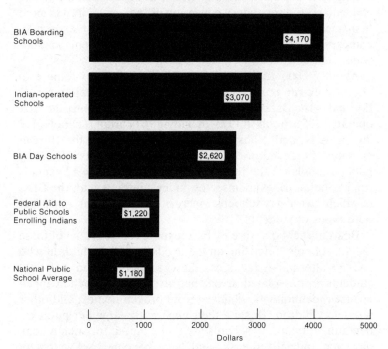

BIA Boarding
Schools $4,170

Indian-operated
Schools $3,070

BIA Day Schools $2,620

Federal Aid to
Public Schools
Enrolling Indians $1,220

National Public
School Average $1,180

0   1000   2000   3000   4000   5000

Dollars

apparently redundant aid, which, in theory at least, has allocated more per Indian child in supplemental funds than the average total expenditure per child in all school districts in the nation. In 1974, public school systems with the responsibility for approximately 135,000 Indian children were slated to receive $52 million in ESEA funds, $42 million in federal aid to impacted areas, and $42 million under the Indian Education Act, in addition to $25 million in Johnson-O'Malley funds. These outlays amounted to a supplement of about $1,200 per Indian child, compared with state and local education funds that averaged about $1,200 per child in fiscal 1973 in the reservations states. The problem, of course, is that not all of these funds

41

actually reach Indian children; they are sometimes diluted among all children in these districts. Still, it appears that the elementary and secondary education of Indian children is more than adequately funded (if not adequately targeted), especially compared with that of other disadvantaged students nationwide.

About 50,000 Indian children live in areas too remote to attend state-run public schools, mostly on the Navajo reservation and in the Dakotas and Alaska. For these students, the BIA operated 195 schools in 1973, including 76 boarding schools, 117 day schools, and 2 hospital schools. In addition, the Bureau operates 19 dormitories housing Indian students attending public schools off the reservation. There were also 12 schools run by Indian tribes themselves under contracts with the BIA, of which 7 were day schools, 2 were boarding schools, and 3 had both types of students.

Boarding schools were by far the most controversial of these federal schools. Focusing on the needs of Indian children who had no alternative facilities, these schools served not only students from isolated areas, but also orphans, handicapped children, delinquents, children from broken homes, and other problem children. Despite their apparently large per-pupil expenditures, boarding schools are understaffed for such a complex and specialized task, and have become backwaters of sub-par education, repeatedly criticized in every official and unofficial report. Part of the problem has clearly been insensitive or overcentralized direction from BIA administrators. With few Indian teachers or administrators and little, if any, parent involvement, the children's needs have been perennially ignored. But even a more responsive and responsible direction from the BIA would not resolve the widely varying needs of the children in boarding schools without increased staffing to provide guidance, special education, and other services.

By contrast, the record of BIA day schools is less criticized. Aimed exclusively at young children—95 percent of the students are in grade school—in remote rural areas, these schools spent more than twice as much per student in fiscal 1972 as the average for public schools in the United States.

One problem that formerly plagued BIA schools, that of attracting and holding qualified teachers, especially Indian teachers, appears to have been alleviated by the teacher surplus in recent years. In 1970, only about one in six teachers in federal schools for Indians were themselves Indians. And the rate of teacher turnover in Indian schools was about 27 percent, or almost double that of public schools nationwide, according to a survey of the years 1964 through 1967. The reasons behind the lack of Indian teachers could be traced to civil service regulations requiring teachers to have a college degree, the longer hours and school years in most districts compared to public schools elsewhere, and the isolated locations of most Indian schools. By 1974, however, more Indians had graduated from colleges, salaries were up, and the BIA reported that it had a backlog of over 100 Indian teachers seeking positions in its school system.[4] The seniority of white teachers and the shrinking size of the federal school system may delay the hiring of these Indian teachers, but in time a much greater proportion of Indians will be hired.

Community Control

The most widely touted development in education has been a transfer of control over a few schools to Indian communities. The initial prototype for these schools was the Rough Rock Demonstration School, established on the Navajo reservation in 1966. Generously funded by the BIA, OEO, and private sources, occupying a new building, and employing freshly recruited and enthusiastic teachers and administrators, the Rough Rock school has been a widely noted success. Encouraged by this success, and prodded by Indian communities who wished to emulate it, the BIA by 1973 had contracted for the operation of twelve schools with various tribal cooperatives and Indian boards of education. Tribes with well-established and competent leadership were allowed to undertake responsibility for planning and administration almost totally independently of the BIA. Although the administrative costs of educating these 2,200 students in contract schools were higher than for more consolidated districts, the positive impacts of involving parents and communities in the educational process apparently outweighed this disadvantage.[5]

Turning complete control of the schools over to the local community is not feasible in all circumstances, especially where tribal organizations are weak or where the school populations are widely dispersed. But legislative and administrative provisions enacted within the past two years have begun to bring Indian parents and organizations into the decision-making processes, even when they have not been given full control. First, the requirement that parent advisory councils be formed in each district that receives Elementary and Secondary Education Act (Title I) funds has given Indian parents a voice (though not veto power) in both federal and public schools. The Indian Education Act of 1972 stipulated that new special programs for Indian children were to be designed and implemented with the full participation of parents and, where possible, of children. Also, in some cases recently, the Johnson-O'Malley funds aiding public school districts with Indian children have been funneled through Indian tribal organizations. As a result of this leverage given to the tribes, these funds have been redirected to projects specifically related to Indian needs. In combination, both measures have begun to redistribute control from national and local bureaucracies to the tribes and Indian communities. Schools that only a few years ago taught American history beginning with Columbus and reading with Dick-and-Jane-in-suburbia stories have become far more sensitive to the needs of Indian education.

Indian education is still beset by many problems, and it remains inadequate in many respects. The custodial mentality still prevails in many boarding schools, with teachers and administrators ignoring the children's needs. The public schools into which increasing proportions of Indian children are being transferred are, in most cases, far more attentive to the requirements of white than Indian students. And though control of schools has been transferred from the BIA to local tribal organizations in some cases, the total dependence of the tribes upon federal funds for their educational systems puts limits on the degree to which educational innovation can be pursued.

But the encouraging developments outweigh the continuing problems. Indians are staying in school longer, graduating from high school more often, and attending college in much greater numbers. More Indians are available to teach in Indian schools. Congressional recognition of Indian educational needs has led to increased federal funding. By 1974, combined state, local, and federal expenditures for Indian elementary and secondary education were more than double the average per student nationwide. Most importantly, the quality of the educational services delivered seemed to be improving, partly as a result of the greater parental and tribal involvement in the educational system brought about by channeling federal assistance funds through Indian organizations.

Aid to Higher Education

According to the most recent estimates, 35 percent of Indian high school graduates go on to college.[6] This percentage is up from about 16 percent in 1950 and 29 percent in 1968, but is still well below rates for whites and blacks, among whom 52 and 43 percent, respectively, of eighteen- and 19-year-old high school graduates were in college in 1972. In large measure, this rise in college enrollment can be traced to greatly increased federal funds made available to college-bound Indian students. In fiscal 1974, the federal government made available to Indian college students approximately $47 million for scholarships, loans, and other subsidies, of which the largest part—$25.8 million, or more than $1,900 per student—was in the form of BIA scholarships for about 13,400 students.

45

BIA scholarships	$25.8
Basic opportunity grants	4.5
Supplementary educational opportunity grants	1.3
Work study	1.5
Subsidized loans	12.6
Direct loans	1.6
TOTAL	$47.3

Although no complete, nonduplicative count of Indian college students has been made, it is estimated that as many as 20,000 Indian college students received a total of more than $50 million in state, tribal, and federal college aid in 1974.[7] With average costs for attendance at public colleges estimated at $2,400 per student in 1974, aid on this scale has clearly put public higher education within reach of many more Indian students than before.

In addition to this aid, the federal government has supported the establishment of several community, vocational, and junior colleges on Indian reservations, the most noted being the recently founded Navajo Community College. Federal funds have paid much of the cost of the construction of the college and, in addition, supply about $2 million annually for operational expenses. The college now has about 300 students enrolled and a staff of 120, with plans for expansion. Courses on all levels (including English as a second language for older students who speak only Navajo) are free to Indians of all ages and are available on a tuition basis to all races. Although it is not operated as a tribal institution, Haskell Junior College in Lawrence, Kansas, also plays an important role in Indian higher education. Here approximately 1,100 Indian students from all over the country take both vocational and junior college courses.

Adult and Vocational Education and Manpower Training

High dropout rates from high school, lower percentages of college attendance, and perennially high unemployment rates make reservation Indians prime candidates for intensive retraining programs after the period of formal education. A number of federal programs are directed to this end, sponsored by the

Departments of Labor, Health, Education, and Welfare, and the Bureau of Indian Affairs. In fiscal 1974, more than $100 million was spent for adult education and training programs, as follows:

Department of Health, Education, and Welfare	$14.6 million
Bureau of Indian Affairs	36.5 million
Department of Labor	50.0 million

Much of this money went to hire or subsidize the hiring of Indians in public and private sector jobs. Smaller, but still substantial sums (estimated at between $10 and $20 million), supported institutional and on-the-job training on and near reservations and maintained a number of other training projects. Nationwide, 2.6 percent of enrollees in Department of Labor manpower programs were Indians.

Beginning with fiscal 1975, manpower training funds are to be available from the Labor Department under the Comprehensive Employment and Training Act. With an estimated $42 million slated to be distributed directly to the tribes for use in manpower efforts as they see fit, this block grant should have a significant impact on orienting manpower programs specifically to Indian needs. All tribes or bands may apply for CETA grants if they have a governing body and a membership of at least 1,000 and are eligible under the Act's formula for an annual grant of at least $50,000. Smaller tribes may pool their membership allocations to receive CETA funds.

The BIA also supports substantial efforts to retrain and reeducate Indians. In fiscal 1973, approximately 11,000 Indians participated in these programs, including 1,200 who received high school equivalency diplomas. In addition, 7,600 students received vocational training of whom about a third completed training, and another third remained enrolled at the year's end. There were also twelve adult learning centers operating on a "drop-in" basis to assist Indians in improving their employability or in furthering their education. Lastly, the Office of Education supports a number of programs in adult and vocational education near Indian reservations. Of special importance are programs that seek to develop professional and paraprofessional teachers, as are grants made to states to operate vocational education centers.

The chief problem with all of these educational upgrading efforts is that they cannot guarantee jobs to even the best-qualified trainees in the depressed labor markets on Indian reservations. Most of the industrial enterprises opening on Indian reservations have been designed to employ low or unskilled employees. Thus, the major sources of job openings for skilled or professional workers are in the government bureaucracies providing social services. Indians who learn skills not applicable to these jobs usually have little choice but to relocate to urban areas to find openings. The BIA actively supports such urban relocation, paying for transportation and transitional support for entire family units. In 1973, more than 5,200 individuals and families received this relocation assistance, at a cost to the government of almost $15 million. Although the emphasis of the program in recent years has shifted toward finding jobs on or near reservations, particularly at newly opened plants, many of the job openings are in urban areas off reservations. Many of the Indians who make these voluntary moves eventually return to the reservations, apparently because the transitional assistance provided by the BIA is insufficient or of too short a duration to overcome the cultural change. Some are assimilated into their urban surroundings, however, thereby easing the labor surplus on the reservations and substantially improving the earnings of these individuals.

Although this program may alleviate the problems of unemployed training graduates, it does not help solve the greater problems of reservation labor markets. With few skilled workers available in the small labor markets on reservations, employers requiring such manpower will not locate there; but without employment possibilities, skilled workers are continually forced to migrate from the reservations to find work, thereby depleting skilled resources in these areas. For this reason, training programs on the reservations will have little effectiveness unless they are tied directly to postgraduation employment opportunities.

4

Health and Family Status

Illnesses and Mortality Rates

The federal government provides free health care through the Indian Health Service to all Indians on and near reservations. Despite this service, Indian health is generally poorer than that of whites and, in some instances, is dramatically worse.

Comparative tables of mortality point up the key problems. Although the Indian population is much younger and therefore has a lower overall death rate, rates adjusted for age indicate that Indians are victims of fatal accidents and most diseases far more often than the population as a whole. Diseases of the heart and malignant neoplasms are a third less common among Indians than among whites. But for each of the other common causes of death, Indians fare considerably worse than the general population, ranging from their five times greater likelihood of death from cirrhosis of the liver to their double risks of diabetes (table 14). A particular problem is accidental death (most often in motor vehicles), which is three times more common among Indians and is the second leading cause of Indian mortality.

In recent years, death rates have dropped for influenza, tuberculosis, enteritis, and congenital diseases. On the other

Table 14. Leading Causes of Death, by Race, 1971 (Rates per 100,000)*

| | Estimated Death Rates | | | Adjusted for age† | | |
	Indian	Nonwhite	White	Indian	Nonwhite	White
Total	772	988	963	936	1,046	694
Major cardiovascular						
diseases	209	412	514	251	458	341
Cirrhosis of the liver	46	19	14	67	24	13
Malignant neoplasms	63	135	163	84	159	127
Influenza and pneumonia	39	43	32	42	42	22
Diabetes	23	24	18	32	28	13
Accidents	157	71	56	183	76	53
(Motor vehicle)	(82)	(30)	(27)	(97)	(34)	(28)
Tuberculosis	8	7	2	11	8	3
Suicide	19	5	12	22	7	12
Homicide	21	34	4	25	41	4
Other	187	238	148	219	203	106

*White data for 1969.
†Using the age distribution of the U.S. population in 1940 as standard.

SOURCE: U.S. Department of Health, Education, and Welfare, Indian Health Service, *Indian Health Trends and Services, 1974* (Washington, D.C.: Government Printing Office, 1974), pp. 32–33; Sar A. Levitan, William B. Johnston, and Robert Taggart, *Still a Dream: The Changing Status of Blacks since 1960* (Cambridge, Mass.: Harvard University Press, 1975).

hand, homicide, suicide, diabetes, and especially cirrhosis of the liver have increased sharply (table 15).

In one area of Indian mortality, the picture appears to be improving steadily. Since 1955, both infant and maternal death rates have dropped, and by 1971 the mortality rates were much closer to those for all races (chart 7). Much of this improvement may be traced to better medical care and the increasing likelihood of hospitalization during childbirth. Since 1955, the proportion of Indian births taking place outside hospitals has fallen from 11.8 to 1.4 percent.

Not only death rates but also incidences of communicable diseases are higher among Indians. In 1971, Indians were far more likely than the general population to contract every disease for which statistics were kept. For diseases such as

Table 15. Percentage of Change in Annual Death Rates of Indians from 1955 to 1971

Accidents	+1
Diseases of the heart	+6
Malignant neoplasms	+6
Cirrhosis of the liver	+221
Diabetes	+65
Homicide	+30
Suicide	+115
Influenza and pneumonia	−57
Diseases of early infancy	−56
Congenital anomalies	−43
Tuberculosis	−86
Enteritis and other diarrheal diseases	−89

SOURCE: U.S. Department of Health, Education, and Welfare, Indian Health Service, *Indian Health Trends and Services, 1974* (Washington, D.C.: Government Printing Office, 1974), p. 32.

mumps, dysentery, hepatitis, venereal disease, tuberculosis, and measles, Indian rates are from four to forty times higher than nationwide averages (table 16). Otitis media, a bacterial ear infection, strikes one in ten Indians (mostly children) annually and is the most common disease among Indians, but it is so rare among the population at large that no national statistics are kept (although studies have found high incidences among other groups in poverty).

Family and Marital Status

Indian social and tribal structures are too diverse to catalog and generalize. Some tribes retain matriarchal lineages or extended clan relationships. Some have adopted democratic institutions, while others are still led by chiefs who inherit their authority. Ancient religious traditions continue to dominate the lives of some tribes, but are completely lost to others. Because of this diversity, statistical indexes of social characteristics may be misleading, and only the most general patterns may be defined.

Indian family structure is more stable than that of other

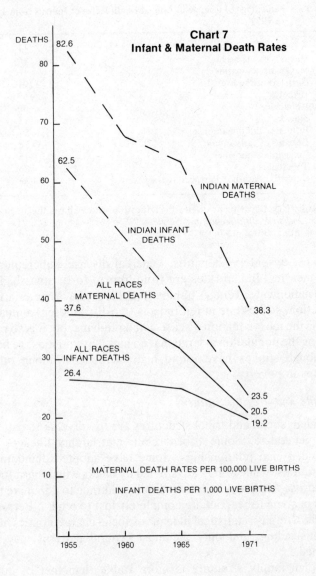

Chart 7
Infant & Maternal Death Rates

DEATHS

INDIAN MATERNAL DEATHS

INDIAN INFANT DEATHS

ALL RACES MATERNAL DEATHS

ALL RACES INFANT DEATHS

MATERNAL DEATH RATES PER 100,000 LIVE BIRTHS

INFANT DEATHS PER 1,000 LIVE BIRTHS

Table 16. Incidence of Leading Communicable Diseases, 1971 (per 1,000 population)

	Indian	All Races
Gonorrhea	16.5	3.2
Mumps	2.9	0.6
Dysentery	4.2	0.1
Hepatitis	3.7	0.3
Syphilis	1.8	0.5
Tuberculosis, new cases	1.6	0.2
Measles	1.6	0.4

SOURCE: U.S. Department of Health, Education, and Welfare, Indian Health Service, *Indian Health Trends and Services, 1974* (Washington, D.C.: Government Printing Office, 1974), p. 51.

minorities, though it stands below white levels on most indexes. In 1970, 18 percent of all Indian families were headed by women, a figure double the rate for whites, but two-thirds of that for blacks. Indian women were more likely than blacks to be married with husbands present, but less likely than whites. On the other hand, Indian families tended to be larger than either those of whites or blacks. Nineteen percent of all Indian families have more than seven persons, compared with 15 percent of black and 5 percent of white families.

	Indian	Black	White
Female-headed families (1970)	18.0%	28.0%	9.0%
Children living with both parents	69.0%	67.0%	91.0%
Women, age 20 and over			
Single	13.0%	15.0%	10.0%
Husband absent, separated, divorced, widowed	27.0%	38.0%	21.0%
Average number of persons per family	4.5	4.1	3.5

One interesting aspect of Indian family status is that it is apparently little affected by the move from the reservation to the city in contrast to the pattern for blacks, in which urban environments correlate with family deterioration. Proportions of female-headed families, women without husbands, and children living with both parents are nearly identical in urban and rural areas. Moreover, urban Indian families have an average of only 3.9 members compared with 4.9 for rural Indian families. Coupled with the greater likelihood of urban Indian families having two or more earners, this suggests that part of the improvement in economic status of urban Indians may be traced to family structure.

Family and Marital Status of Indians, 1970

	Urban	Rural
Female-headed families	19%	18%
Women, age 20 and over		
Single	13%	12%
Husband absent, divorced,		
widowed, separated	28%	25%
Children living with both		
parents	67%	70%
Number of persons per		
family	3.9	4.9
Families with 7 or more		
members	11%	26%

Moreover, there is little evidence of the rapid trend toward deterioration of the family unit such as has been observed for other minorities. Over the decade of the 1960s, the proportion of female-headed families crept up only 2 percentage points, while the proportion of women who were single, widowed, divorced, or separated actually declined.

Birth Rates and Age Distribution

Indians have the highest rate of natural increase of any of the population subgroups in the United States—3 percent per year (chart 8). At this rate, their population more than doubles every generation, despite the average life expectancy of approximately six years less than that of the population as a whole. In 1970, the number of Indian children born per thousand Indian women ages fifteen to forty-four (the fertility rate) was 155,

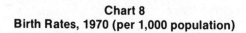

Chart 8
Birth Rates, 1970 (per 1,000 population)

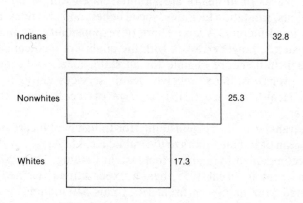

Indians   32.8

Nonwhites   25.3

Whites   17.3

nearly double the white rate of 84 and a third higher than the nonwhite rate of 114. These high rates mean that reservation Indians are, on the average, much younger than the population in general, with the median age of eighteen compared to twenty-eight for all persons in 1970. In terms of dependency ratios, this means that for each potential Indian male breadwinner between the ages of twenty-five and fifty-four years, there are 4.1 potential dependents under nineteen years of age, while for the population as a whole, there are 2.2 potential dependents. Already economically disadvantaged, reservation Indians have, on the average, twice as many mouths to feed.

It is improbable that this youthful and expanding population structure will change much in the near future. While both white and nonwhite birth rates have dropped steadily since the 1950s, the Indian rate has fallen more slowly from its peak in the early 1960s. The large numbers of Indian women reaching childbearing age, plus continued improvements in health care that will lengthen Indian life spans, can be expected to boost population growth over the next decade.

Indian Health Service

The causes of ill health are an interrelated web of housing conditions, sanitation facilities, social beliefs and practices, and institutional factors. A large share of responsibility for Indian health status, however, rests with the quality of medical care. Although Indians are eligible for all state, local, and federal health programs, most receive health services through the Indian Health Service (IHS), an arm of the Public Health Service.

The transfer of the responsibility for Indian health care from the Bureau of Indian Affairs to the Public Health Service in 1955 was accompanied by a sharp increase in funding. From $24.5 million spent in fiscal 1955, health expenditures reached an estimated $168 million in fiscal 1973, plus $49 million for the construction of new hospitals, community facilities, personnel quarters, and sanitation facilities. Two-thirds of the operational money was spent for patient care in IHS hospitals and other medical facilities. Another $50 million went for field health services (table 17).

The IHS operates fifty-one hospitals (with a combined capacity of about 2,700 beds), all of which also offer outpatient services. In addition, the wide dispersal of Indian population requires the IHS to contract for medical care with community hospitals, clinics, private physicians, and dentists. These services are especially needed for specialized medical attention, since few specialists are attracted to IHS service.

The IHS supports a number of ancillary health programs. Under the Sanitation Facilities Construction Act, running water and waste disposal systems have been provided to a total of 78,000 reservation homes and community buildings. Corrective dental treatment, such as fillings and dentures, and preventive measures, such as water fluoridation and fluoride treatment, are available at or provided for by IHS facilities. Public health nurses in Indian communities and educational programs in schools encourage Indian use and acceptance of medical care.

Table 17. Expenditures for Indian Health in Fiscal 1973 (in Millions)

Patient care			$114.2
IHS hospitals		$83.3	
Contractual services		30.9	
Hospitalization	$16.5		
Physicians and dental services	9.9		
Other services	4.5		
Field health services			50.2
Sanitation		7.2	
Dental		6.1	
Public health nursing		3.8	
Health education		1.7	
Field medical services		31.4	
Administration			3.4
Construction			48.6
TOTAL			$216.5

SOURCE: U.S. Congress, House, *Department of the Interior and Related Agencies Appropriations for 1974, Part 4, Hearings* before a subcommittee of the Committee on Appropriations, 93d Cong., 1st sess. (Washington, D.C.: Government Printing Office, 1973), pp. 44–45, 95.

Other programs operate primarily through satellite health centers and traveling clinics focusing on local needs. These may be oriented toward communicable diseases, alcoholism, nutrition, or family planning. In view of the great population pressure on Indian reservations, family planning efforts are particularly important. In 1972, approximately 20,000 Indian women were accepting birth control assistance, slightly more than a fifth of the female population from fifteen to forty-four years of age.

All told, the IHS employs about 7,500 personnel in all its health programs, including 490 physicians, 180 dentists, and 1,100 registered nurses. Though the numbers of these trained health workers have risen faster than the Indian population in recent years, expert medical care is still spread more thinly among Indians than among the general population. Measured in terms of practicing professionals per ten thousand persons, the distribution in 1971 was:

	Indians	*All Races*
Physicians	10.1	13.9
Dentists	2.9	4.7
Registered nurses	22.8	35.6

The IHS has not been able to enlist more medical professionals because of the remote and unattractive reservation locations, limited facilities, and lower relative pay scales. Most physicians and dentists received salaries of less than $20,000 from the IHS in 1971, compared to median earnings of more than double that among doctors in private practice. Since the end of the Vietnam era, when physicians could perform service in the IHS in lieu of being drafted into the military, the recruitment problem has become worse. Although the earnings differential is not so drastic for nurses, the lack of social life and other amenities on reservations creates perennial shortages of registered nurses in IHS hospitals and health centers.

In response to this problem and in an attempt to raise the numbers of Indians employed in these professional health occupations, the IHS has encouraged the enrollment of Indians in medical, dental, and nursing programs. Although there were only 2 Indian doctors and 13 Indian professional nurses in the Indian Health Service in 1972, there were 74 Indians in medical and dental schools and almost 500 in nursing programs (though there is no guarantee these trainees will enter service with the IHS). In addition, Indian employment in and training for the medical specialties, such as technician, hygienist, and therapist, is also increasing. In 1972, 500 Indians enrolled in various technical medical training programs.

Along with efforts to develop Indian medical professionals and in line with the federal policy of turning greater responsibility for Indian affairs over to the tribes, the IHS has sought to contract with various Indian governments and agencies for the delivery of some health services. In particular, many of the special programs, clinics, and local health centers concerned with immunization, infant care, family planning, alcoholism, venereal diseases, otitis media, and trachoma have been established under tribal auspices. A number of tribes have established Indian health boards that direct and coordinate the delivery of all health services on the reservations.

Another facet of the self-determination effort in health care is the funding of tribally employed community health workers. In remote areas such as Alaska, these nonprofessional workers may provide the only available medical care. In other areas, their function is to act as the liaison between community residents and the IHS or other health agencies and to encourage the use of available health resources. In 1973, there were about 900 such workers employed by the tribes, and a total of approximately $15 million was being funneled into tribally controlled health programs.

The Impact of the Indian Health Service

Indian usage of the medical care available to them has been rising. As the older tribal members die, both the practitioners of and believers in traditional medicine have diminished. The education programs mounted by the IHS, especially the tribally employed community health workers, have had an increasing impact. Both admissions to hospitals and outpatient visits have surged during the past two decades. The rate of hospital utilization (per 100 persons) actually surpassed that of the general population in 1972.

	Indians	*All Races*
Hospitalizations	22	16
Physician outpatient visits	476	490

Part of this higher rate of hospital utilization may be traced to the continuing problem areas of Indian health. The three leading causes of Indian hospitalizations are deliveries and complications of pregnancy; accidents, poisonings, and violence; and diseases of the respiratory system—all problems far more common among Indians than among others.

Improved and more frequent dental care is also evident. In 1972, two-fifths of all eligible Indians received dental services, twice the proportion as in 1955. The IHS has properly concentrated its services on youths, and 55 percent of those under age forty received dental care in 1972. Of all dental services estimated to be required by children between the ages of five and fourteen, 72 percent were performed. The impact of these dental efforts can be seen in the results of dental examinations of youths between the ages of six and seventeen. Tabulations by the IHS show that in 1957 only 28 percent of all "problem" teeth of children examined by IHS dentists had received fillings. In 1972, 54 percent had had this corrective treatment.

On balance, there can be no question that the stepped-up federal health expenditures have made impressive improvements in Indian health. Death in childbirth or infancy and the incidence of tuberculosis, pneumonia, enteritis, trachoma, and dental problems are all down, while hospitalization, physician and dental visits, health education, and sanitation engineering have been upgraded. The health problems with clearly defined causes, amenable to prevention and treatment, have been sharply curtailed. Indian health provides a clear case in which increased federal investments in social welfare have had a significant payoff.

On the other hand, the one continuing serious and relatively unattacked health problem is alcohol abuse. Although the published raw data do not show the interrelationship, the most important common thread that seems to unite the rising rates and higher likelihood of certain causes of death is alcohol. Accidents, suicides, homicides, and cirrhosis of the liver have been reported by the Indian Health Service to be commonly alcohol-related. Each of these problems have been on the rise since federal laws prohibiting the sale of liquor to Indians were repealed in 1953. At the same time, social problems reported to be related to alcohol, such as abandonment and crime, have also increased. If all alcohol-related deaths were lumped together, it is possible that they would account for more than a fourth of Indian mortality.

The seriousness of this problem has been compounded by the relatively complacent attitude of both the IHS and the tribal councils. For example, in the 1974 appropriations hearings, the IHS benignly argued that "chronic addictive type alcoholism is not much more prevalent among Indians than among Americans generally," and Dr. Emory Johnson, director of the IHS, suggested that new tribal willingness to face and deal with the problem was a hopeful sign.[1] Though a number of alcohol clinics and prevention programs have been established, the problem has not been solved by these measures but continues to grow worse. It does little service to the Indian community to raise the tired explanations of "difficulties adjusting to the white man's world," or to assume that the problems can be solved by funding a few alcohol abuse clinics. If the rising trend of Indian alcohol addiction is to be arrested, the problem must be confronted with direct research into its biological and social causes, followed by extensive rehabilitation efforts. Until such efforts are mounted, the otherwise exemplary improvements in Indian health will be Pyrrhic victories.

5

Social Services

In addition to programs for economic development, education, and health care, the federal government has assumed responsibility for many other social needs on Indian reservations. Federal programs fund indigent families, housing, and police protection, as well as the development of tribal governments and the establishment of community organizations. And a federal bureaucracy manages Indian tribal assets and lands. All told, the BIA and other agencies spent in fiscal 1974, $253 million to deliver social services for Indians.

		(Millions)
<u>TOTAL</u>		<u>$253.1</u>
BIA		$107.2
Indian services	$ 92.5	
Trust responsibilities	$ 14.7	
Veterans Administration		$ 16.8
HUD		$ 18.9
HEW		$110.2
Public assistance	$ 79.3	
Office of Native American		
Programs	$ 30.9	

Public Assistance

Direct payments to support Indian families, children, and retired and disabled workers accounted for the bulk of social service outlays. Widespread poverty and unemployment on reservations make large proportions of Indian families eligible for federal and state public assistance programs. In recent years growing awareness of these programs and liberalized eligibility requirements have dramatically expanded caseloads and costs. In 1968, approximately 88,000 Indians received assistance; by 1973, the figure was over 157,000, or about 28 percent of all Indians on or near reservations. Federal expenditures for these programs, of course, have also expanded, from about $46 million in 1968 to about $126 million in 1973.

Until recently, most of the public assistance given to Indians came under categorical programs administered and partly funded by the states and localities. In 1974 aid to the blind, the aged, and the disabled was completely taken over by the federal government, leaving only aid to families with dependent children still partly funded by the states. The states and localities have not been eager, however, to extend welfare assistance to reservations, since Indians contribute proportionately small amounts to local tax revenues. As a result, many Indians do not qualify under stringent state standards. For families and individuals ineligible for categorical programs, the BIA provides, as do most states, general welfare assistance. Though this general assistance has grown at a rapid pace (doubling every five years between 1960 and 1970, and tripling from 1970 to 1973), the aid still did not compare in 1973 with that available under categorical programs (chart 9).

Part of the BIA general assistance is in the form of subsidized employment. Under this program, which is administered by the tribes under contracts with the BIA, heads of households who volunteer are employed to perform needed work such as home construction and repair, building maintenance, and the development of recreational facilities. Participants are paid $40 a

Chart 9
Public Assistance on Reservations, 1973

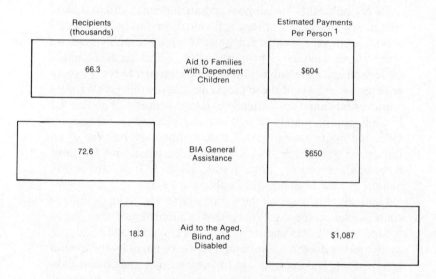

Recipients (thousands)		Estimated Payments Per Person [1]
66.3	Aid to Families with Dependent Children	$604
72.6	BIA General Assistance	$650
18.3	Aid to the Aged, Blind, and Disabled	$1,087

[1] Average benefit levels in 10 states with largest Indian population

month by the tribes (who are reimbursed by the BIA) in addition to their assistance payments. Total costs for 4,250 participants in thirty tribal programs in fiscal 1974 amounted to $2.4 million.

Indians also received support from a number of other sources, including veterans' benefits, social security, and unemployment insurance. Although the likelihood of Indians receiving such payments is less and the size of their stipends is smaller than national averages, these sources of income add considerably to reservation income. Total welfare payments accounted for about $200 million in fiscal 1974, and may now account for as much as a fifth of Indian income.

Housing

Indian reservations have been aptly characterized as "open air slums."[1] In 1973, the BIA housing survey found that out of

107,000 Indian families, 66,000 needed housing assistance. Of these, 19,000 lived in homes that could be brought up to standards by renovation, and 47,000 lived in shelters so dilapidated or overcrowded that they required new homes.[2] According to the 1970 census, 44 percent of all rural Indian households lived in housing with more than one person per room. Half had no bathroom, and a third lacked any interior water supply. One-third of all rural Indian households lived in homes more than thirty years old, and two-thirds of all dwellings were valued at less than $7,500.[3] These housing conditions were far worse than for the rest of the population, black or white. For example, only 19 percent of black families lived more than one person per room, and only 16 percent lived in homes without adequate plumbing.

Both the BIA and the Department of Housing and Urban Development (HUD) operate programs aimed at improving these conditions. Since 1961, federal law has allowed Indian tribes to establish housing authorities that can obtain financing for low-rent public housing, turnkey, and mutual help construction projects. Low-rent public housing and turnkey programs have operated much as in other areas, with HUD supplying supplements to low-income families, which allow them to rent or purchase dwellings built with federally backed financing. In addition to these conventional types of housing programs, HUD, in conjunction with the BIA, operates an unusual mutual help housing and construction program that supplies a small number of homes for purchase by Indians. Under the mutual help program, Indians may build or help to build homes in which they use their "sweat equity" as a down payment. With total costs thus lowered and the government subsidizing a long-term mortgage, the owner-builder may move into his house by paying as little as $7 per month to cover administrative costs. Thereafter, if his income rises, his payments may increase in order to amortize the loan over approximately twenty-five years. Under this and other HUD housing programs, approximately 6,000 housing units were constructed in fiscal 1974.

The BIA also operates a housing improvement program

aimed at constructing and renovating Indian homes. In 1974, the BIA spent approximately $13 million to remodel 4,400 homes and to construct about 500 new ones. Altogether, federal housing assistance reached about 11,000 families in fiscal 1974, or about one-sixth of those estimated to be in need.

Insufficient funds are only one obstacle to providing adequate housing for the worst-housed Indians. Many of these families lack the know-how, the resources, and sometimes the inclination to keep their housing in proper repair. Another difficulty is that most Indians prefer ownership to rental—60 percent of all Indian homes are owner-occupied, and on reservations the figure may reach 80 percent. Many Indians resist moving from their tar-paper shacks into new rental housing on which even the low monthly payments may seem exorbitant. As with public housing efforts in other areas, programs for Indians need to include social and educational services to see that the new buildings meet the needs of the people who are to occupy them, and that projects are cared for to ensure that they do not become newly constructed slums.

Law Enforcement

On most Indian reservations, the tribe has jurisdiction over minor crimes committed by and against Indians that carry penalties of less than six months in jail or a $500 fine. Some reservations leave all law enforcement responsibility to the state or county. Since few tribal governments have incomes sufficient to support the personnel, equipment, and facilities needed to operate complete police, judicial, and penal systems, the BIA supports these activities. In fiscal 1974 approximately $8.8 million went to support law enforcement. These funds paid 177 police officers, staffed twenty-three detention centers, and supplied prevention, rehabilitation, and parole services on eighty-seven reservations. In addition, many tribes contributed some or most of their own support for law enforcement—most notably the Navajos, who paid for 90 percent of a program costing more than $3 million. Altogether, BIA and tribal support for law enforcement totaled about $13.3 million.

Several of the tribes who have taken over financial responsibility for law enforcement in previous years are now petitioning the federal government for more help. Faced with lower tribal income, the Navajos and the San Carlos Apaches have asked the BIA for increased funding. In this case, at least, the price of self-determination has become too high to afford.

For many types of crimes, law enforcement problems on Indian reservations are greater than those in other rural areas. Overall, Indian rates for the seven most serious crimes were about 63 percent greater than for the rural population as a whole.[4] Crimes of violence (in rates per 100,000 persons) are far more common among Indians, while property crimes are less than half as likely among Indians as among other rural Americans (table 18).

One common element that underlies the problems of crime on reservations is alcohol abuse. In 1970, alcohol-related crimes accounted for about two-fifths of all reported offenses. In particular, the astronomical rate for aggravated assault—twenty times that for whites in urban areas and more than twice the black urban rate—may be traced to alcohol. As with alcohol-related health problems, alcohol-related crimes need to be attacked at the cause rather than the symptom, with more funds spent for prevention, rehabilitation, and treatment rather than simply for law enforcement.

Trust Responsibilities and Services

Over the years, many Indian tribes have built up substantial trust funds, which are held by the federal government for the benefit of tribal members. Initially, these funds were payments for rights to Indian lands. More recently, the chief increments to the trusts have come from payments made by the Indian Claims Commission (which had made awards totaling $468 million through mid-1974) and from income from trust lands ($75 million in 1974). Because of concern that financially unsophisticated Indian leaders might lose these assets, the BIA has been charged with managing and investing them. For many years this consisted of leaving the money in the U.S. Treasury, where it

Table 18. Comparative Crime Rates (per 100,000 population)

	BIA	All Rural Areas
Murder	19.0	6.4
Rape	47.9	9.9
Aggravated assault	972.9	89.6
Robbery	8.0	14.1
Burglary	241.2	434.0
Larcency over $50	104.4	302.7
Auto theft	80.6	70.7

received 4 percent interest. Since 1966, however, funds have been more aggressively invested, with more than 90 percent of the $330 million in tribal funds now placed in banks and securities. The total Indian portfolio managed by the BIA yielded about 6½ percent in 1973. In addition to these tribally owned trusts, the BIA also manages approximately $130 million in private Indian funds. Most of these personal trust services are unregulated accounts holding nonearned income from leases, awards, and other sources for Indians living far from banking facilities. A few, however, are controlled accounts for Indians deemed incompetent to handle their affairs.

The BIA also performs a number of real estate services in connection with Indian trust land, including lease processing, appraisals, surveys, and title conveyance services. These services accounted for more than seven-eighths of the $14 million the BIA spent to manage Indian trust lands and money in 1973. Since returns from leased land are a sizable proportion of Indian income, real estate services are vitally important to many tribes. Recently, there have been an increasing number of disputes concerning the provisions and rates of return in leases negotiated in earlier years by the BIA, and the tribes are now taking a more active part in the management of their real estate.

The federal role in managing Indian property poses difficult questions. On one hand, many Indian tribes and individuals are not financially sophisticated enough to invest their money wisely. Others prefer to be free of the trouble of managing their finances and are glad they do not have to pay financial advisors to perform services now done by the BIA for free. Some tribes, however, object to the veto power that the BIA holds over decisions concerning their investments. To satisfy these complaints, it appears that a system of voluntary trust management is warranted.

On the other hand, if the BIA is to have some control and influence over Indian money, more leverage should be exerted to encourage Indian investment in the development of their reservations. Most tribal leaders have been unwilling or unable to commit funds to projects for economic or community development. Often older or poorer tribal members prefer short-term disbursement to long-term projects, and thus more than a third of tribal income is simply paid out on a per capita basis. Moreover, Indian leaders are generally conservative regarding investments, preferring to buy more land (often with low returns) rather than to put funds into business or community enterprises, which eventually might have higher returns and reduce unemployment. Few Indians have the experience or expertise needed to run business enterprises, and the factors weighing against reservation locations make the prospects for high or even break-even returns from Indian enterprises doubtful. But ultimately, Indian self-determination must be founded on financial self-reliance. Unless Indian funds are committed to projects administered by Indians to benefit and employ Indians, much of their potential has been wasted, no matter what interest rate they may draw on deposit in local banks.

Community Development and Tribal Self-Determination

At the opposite pole from the BIA paternalistic control over Indian trusts are efforts to stimulate tribal participation in and control over Indian affairs. Self-determination for Indians basically involves two processes: (1) establishing and developing tribal governments and organizations; and (2) turning budgetary, administrative, and operational control of Indian programs over to these Indian agencies. Additionally, self-determination involves an attitude on the part of the federal government that commits it to consider the wishes and priorities of the tribes in administering programs funded by the government.

Under the Tribal Government Development Program, the BIA provided about $10.9 million in aid to tribal governments in 1974. These funds supported tribal government operations and paid for costs of providing technical assistance to tribal governments to improve the quality of their services, including planning and participation in BIA budget formulation deliberations. These functions included the preparation of tribal judgment rolls (determining who was eligible for payments from the Indian Claims Commission), explanation and interpretation of government services and programs available, and the preparation of new charters, constitutions, and legal codes.

A related effort, originally funded by the Office of Economic Opportunity, to develop Indian communities is supported by the Office of Native American Programs (ONAP) within the Department of Health, Education, and Welfare. ONAP supplies advice, assistance, and financial support to community action agencies on Indian reservations and in Indian urban areas. Grants are made directly to tribal governments or to established Indian organizations for programs such as community organization, neighborhood and health centers, and manpower training. ONAP spent in fiscal 1974 about $31 million to support programs serving 157 reservations and 54 urban areas. Most funds were channeled directly to tribal units for programs designed specifically to meet Indian needs, with only a small amount supporting national programs.

Legal services, another OEO-sponsored community action program, apparently has had a definite impact on developing awareness of tribal and individual rights, although only $1.5 million was available in fiscal 1973 to support the program on eight reservations. Most program services provided aid for

70

individuals with legal problems. But in some cases, antipoverty lawyers have helped bring about social and administrative change. For example, legal aides are credited with improving the rate of Indian utilization of welfare benefits in many states where bureaucracies were not eager to provide assistance to untaxed Indians. Similarly, the legal service program has occasionally fought to ensure that federal money earmarked for Indian education is not diluted in programs for other children. A more recent program of legal assistance is funded by the Law Enforcement Assistance Administration, which provides legal, procedural, and administrative instruction to tribal court judges.

Strengthening tribal governments and providing legal assistance are not the only steps being taken toward Indian self-determination. The more important phase of self-determination is the turning over of responsibilities to Indians, especially control of the purse strings. This policy of divesting monetary control has proceeded slowly. Twelve schools are fully operated by Indians under contracts with the BIA, and about a third of funds to aid public schools are funneled through the tribes. Tribal organizations have undertaken contracts for community health organizations, police responsibility, and some manpower training and direct employment programs. Altogether, the BIA estimates that about 22 percent of its fiscal 1974 budget went directly to contracts or grants to Indians. This figure, however, exaggerates the true amount of financial control that has been delegated to Indians. Most of the $124 million listed under contracts and grants to Indians consisted of welfare payments, scholarships, and direct employment support. Most federal schools, health services, social welfare aid, and resource development are still handled and controlled by the federal government.

6

"The Indian Question"

Underlying Facts

Ever since the Indians were placed on reservations more than a hundred years ago, federal officials have been attempting to "solve the Indian question." The apparent order and simplicity of confining a group of people to a limited land area made the problem seem deceptively clear. Through various eras, politicians have seized on a succession of "obvious" single-word solutions: assimilation, support, termination, and more recently self-determination. But no policy, slogan, or program has succeeded in rectifying the initial mistake of uprooting Indians from their lands and forcing them to live on the most barren, resourceless, unproductive lands that no settlers wanted.

There are still no answers to "the Indian question." Indians themselves are often bitterly divided as to what their status should be, given the inevitable conflicts between the traditional life on reservations and the prevailing social and economic values of American society. Several facts stand out, however.

1. The problems of Indians are better termed the problems of reservations. Off the reservation, Indians are better off than other American minorities, though they still suffer by compari-

son with whites. It is those who elect to remain or who are stranded on tribal lands who face the most severe economic, educational, health, and social problems.

2. In terms of the reservation conditions which can be improved through heavy government expenditures, substantial progress has been made. Indian health care, educational facilities and enrollment, social welfare, and housing on the reservation have been upgraded, though critics would charge that the improvement has not been nearly fast enough. But with federal spending for these services at more than a billion dollars per year, it appears that Indian needs are no longer slighted compared to those of other needy segments of American society. Sustained funding at these levels should begin to alleviate problems related to poverty, unemployment, poor education, and poor health.

3. Although continuing heavy funding may quiet the critics by raising standards of living on reservations, money will not resolve the more difficult remaining problems. These thorny issues have to do with fundamental cultural differences and with the basic status of Indians on reservations. The economic independence that most planners concede must be a prerequisite to true Indian self-determination is nowhere in sight. This is not only a problem of lacking resources—human and natural—and of insufficient technical assistance. Indians, whose values were not attuned to competitive capitalist economics, were ill-prepared to pursue aggressively success in agriculture, business, or industry, even if they had been offered the opportunity. A century of dependence on the federal government has exacerbated rather than alleviated this problem. To a great degree, Indians remain culturally unprepared to be economically independent.

Whatever steps are taken to ameliorate Indian conditions must reckon with the evident conflict between the rhetoric of self-determination and the inevitable reality of federal control of the purse strings. The disputes between militants who want total independence, and older tribal leaders, who fear "termination," represent a basic conflict that cannot be resolved to everyone's satisfaction. Both sides see opposite ends of the same federal elephant—one, the all-powerful "oppressor" holding total financial and bureaucratic control over Indian lives, the other, the provider of services and the guarantor of Indian sovereignty over their own lands and governments. To some, reservations themselves appear to be the greatest obstacle standing in the way of Indian independence, since they so drastically hinder economic and educational progress. Yet, to others, reservations are enclaves of remaining independence and the link to Indian tribal traditions, language, and tribal identity. To some degree, it appears something must be lost no matter how Indians approach self-determination.

Policy Considerations

Even though the ultimate directions and specific implementations of federal policies should be decided by Indians, the federal government must continue an active and influential role on Indian reservations for the foreseeable future. The complex history and continuing problems of Indians on reservations precludes any dramatic reversals or reconsiderations of most federal programs. Treaty obligations cannot be swept away with new legislation, and neither can the federal role in providing education, health, welfare, and resource development and management services be abandoned. Though the pace of progress—especially that toward Indian self-determination—may seem maddeningly slow to many Indians and to others, there is no "quick fix," even if enormously greater resources are made available. The perspective must be long-term, and the results may not be visible in year-to-year evaluations.

Thus, many of the immediate courses of federal action must be categorized as more of the same—more federal aid for health, welfare, and education; a continued slow shift of authority over policy and budgeting to the tribes; stepped up management and technical assistance. On the other hand, there are some new directions that federal policy might take.

Status off the Reservations   Immediate attention should be given to modifying the long-standing practice of placing geographic limits on the availability of services to Indians. This policy may have been justified a century ago, when the last treaty with Indian tribes was signed and most Indians were confined to reservations; and it is still reasonable for the BIA to focus primarily on reservation Indians, since their problems are most severe. But with an increasingly mobile Indian population, many of whom are leaving reservations, it is unrealistic to draw tight boundaries around Indian services. At a minimum, the BIA should be authorized to expand greatly the availability and scope of services to Indians in urban areas. Where large numbers of urban Indians reside, a "branch office" should be authorized to provide placement services, continued health care, access to, and information about, local welfare and other assistance programs, and other kinds of temporary help. Even if the primary focus of policy is to encourage the development and independence of Indian reservations, it makes little sense to require Indians to sink or swim if they decide to leave the reservation.

Indian Education   As has been suggested, the funds available for Indian education appear to be adequate. What is needed now is consolidation of the federal spigots coupled with greater Indian control and involvement in the federal funding process to assure that the resources are directly and wisely spent on the education of Indian children. While the details of the steps toward this goal will vary in different areas of the country, depending on whether local, tribal, or federal schools predominate, all systems should seek to shift control of the schools, including funding, staffing, and choice of curriculum, to Indian educators and parents.

One key to this process must be the staffing of Indian schools—both local and federal—with Indian teachers. As growing numbers of Indians graduate from college and more well-educated Indians from urban areas opt for returning to reservations, there is no reason to maintain predominantly non-Indian staffs in schools with large numbers of Indian children. Slow teacher turnover and local prejudice may retard the hiring of Indian teachers, but every federal and tribal pressure should be brought to accelerate the process.

Health Care   The supply of Indian elementary and secondary schoolteachers may increase, but the numbers of professional Indians in the health care system may not rise without more active efforts by the federal government. Proposals in Congress to subsidize the higher education of greater numbers of Indian medical personnel are one step that should be taken. More use could also be made of paraprofessionals to perform routine duties; training for these positions should be supplied in reservation manpower training programs.

Long training times mean that it may be several years before significant numbers of Indians will be available to staff the Indian Health Service; meanwhile, immediate action is necessary to ensure that adequate numbers of medical specialists, whether Indian or not, are available to fill all authorized slots in IHS institutions. The doctors who flocked to Indian reservations to perform alternative service in lieu of the military draft during the Vietnam war have now mostly departed, leaving many hospitals critically short of staff. The current federal salary structure and regulations are major obstacles to attracting physicians and other health professionals to reservation medical facilities. More flexible salary and other incentives are necessary to bring adequate numbers of doctors and nurses to reservations.

Finally, the federal government should appropriate sufficient money to the IHS to allow it to do large-scale research into the etiology of and therapy for Indian alcoholism. No other health problem deserves higher priority.

Employment Assistance   Manpower programs on Indian reservations should be completely geared to the job market, and no training should be undertaken without a specific employment objective. This means, first, that a majority of those in reservation training programs should be oriented toward positions in the health, education, welfare, or technical assistance bureaucracies supported by the federal government. Although 62 percent of current employees of the BIA are Indians, this percentage should rise overall, and especially in the professional and managerial categories. Secondly, programs that seek to relocate Indians to jobs and training in urban areas should not be abandoned, but should be available to those who want them. This assistance should be far more intensive than it is at present, including lengthy training and extended assistance and follow-up to ease the transitional process. A small number of successes are preferable to large numbers who return to the reservation more hopeless than before.

Obviously, neither of these steps, nor economic development efforts on the reservations, is soon likely to absorb a large proportion of the Indian unemployed. This role should be undertaken by a substantial federally supported public employment program. Indisputably, there are badly needed public projects to be implemented on reservations—housing, sanitation, and roads and other transportation facilities, among others—and thousands of idle workers. During the lengthy period of economic development on reservations, a sustained program of public works projects should be undertaken to utilize and develop these idle resources. Given the depressed status of reservations, the cost per job of the program would be low, and the overall magnitude of the effort would not have to be large to have a significant impact; a $50 million program could hire more Indians than the total employed in all economic development projects currently operating. Especially for older unskilled workers, who are unlikely candidates for extensive training or relocation, public works projects could be beneficial not only to the idle workers who would be hired but also to the reservations.

Development of Tribal Governments   The fledgling program of tribal government development currently under way needs to be expanded and accelerated. The most important step should be the encouragement of greater participation by tribal members in political and tribal activities. While the democratic tradition is not endemic to all tribes, several of the recent disputes between militant and traditional Indians have stemmed from dissatisfaction with established governing elites. One cure for entrenched power groups is fuller participation by more informed tribal members. This goal might be furthered if the BIA supported the development of tribal newspapers or radio stations. For example, Indian radio stations broadcasting a few hours a day of news, music, and educational programs might do much to educate and inform Indians scattered over reservations, inducing greater participation and sense of belonging in tribal affairs.

A second aspect of tribal development should be the recruitment and hiring of technical advisers to the tribes. These individuals, whose skills might range from financial management to range development, should provide the tribes with the in-house expertise now supplied by the BIA. Most importantly, these positions should be temporary, offering training to tribal members to establish their own training and development programs once they gain the necessary experience and expertise. While such complete transfer of responsibilities is not yet feasible for all tribes, it should be vigorously pursued wherever possible. For decades federal policy has vacillated between "doing it for them" and "letting them do it for themselves." But not enough sustained effort has been devoted to developing expertise in resource management among Indians themselves.

Economic Development   The future of Indian reservations depends on self-sustaining economic growth. Ultimately, all efforts to assist tribal development and self-determination must be considered paternalism unless Indian resources and enterprises generate employment and wealth in Indian hands. Given the dearth of human and natural resources on most reservations, the lack of a business infrastructure, and the difficulty of amassing sufficient momentum to sustain economic growth, the process of building reservation economies must be expected to take decades or generations. This long-term program can be aided most by realistic decisions, long-term planning, and substantial federal investments.

1. The focus of the most intensive development projects should be reservations with the greatest potential for developing human and natural resources. Reservations with an adequate population base and with timber, mineral, or other resources have the best chance of developing integrated viable industrial systems. This strategy may seem to be one of helping the rich to get richer, but it is unrealistic to expect an industrial park in a remote desert, unsupported by any natural advantages, to generate continued growth after the various incentives for businesses are ended.

2. In line with the development of reservations with the greatest resources, the inventories of natural and water resources currently under way on Indian reservations should be accelerated. The development of Indian reservations may require many years, but there is no need to delay the process by postponing and prolonging the research and planning phases.

3. Tribes with substantial financial resources should be encouraged to invest them in economic development projects. Some system of matching federal grants or loan guarantees might help free conservatively held tribal funds. Another use of tribal money would be the repurchase of sold and leased Indian lands. In some areas, where Indian landholdings have been checkerboarded into inefficient parcels, a program to develop largely tribally owned cooperative farms with federal loans or grants might be warranted.

4. Long-term government contracts should be more actively utilized on reservations with few natural resources. The $125-million five-year contract let to the Devils Lake Sioux Manufacturing Corporation by the Department of Defense is an example of ensured profitability guaranteeing the viability of an Indian enterprise. Of course, there are many depressed areas of the country vying for such deals. There are, however, powerful arguments that reservations have the most depressed conditions and the least prospect for attracting private industry, and

thus are most deserving of these long-term contracts. Other areas are likely to suffer only temporary job deficits, while the depressed economic conditions on reservations are chronic and are likely to remain so without such special assistance.

5. Industry which employs Indians should certainly be encouraged to locate on reservations, but emphasis should also be placed on Indian ownership of the small retail outlets that already exist on and near reservations. These grocery stores, gas stations, restaurants, and other small businesses are often owned by non-Indians. A concerted effort should be made to place Indian entrepreneurs in these small enterprises. This effort should include loans, planning, and technical assistance on a long-term basis, and should not be deterred by high initial failure rates. In some cases, the tribes themselves may operate the enterprises, but for many small stores and similar establishments, the profits are barely sufficient to sustain one family. No matter how small the business, however, it is preferable that Indians rather than non-Indians should reap the gains.

None of the indicated policy shifts is likely to produce immediate results, nor is it even certain that the suggested options will yield long-term gains. The process of building Indian "nations" will inevitably take many years, especially since it must be fundamentally guided and motivated by tribal initiatives. As earnestly as federal officials may want to solve the problems with appropriations, or as much as a compassionate or guilt-ridden public may want to lend a hand, non-Indians can only be limited "nonvoting" partners in the process of Indian development and self-determination. Ultimately, Indians must decide the future course of their culture. Federal policy, a chain of mistakes and tragedies extending almost to the present, must at last leave the resolution of "the Indian question" to Indians.

Notes

Chapter 1

1. The two major sources of data on Indians, the U.S. Bureau of the Census and the Bureau of Indian Affairs, use different definitions and methods of collecting their statistics. The census counts all Indians who identify themselves as such. The Bureau of Indian Affairs ignores those who do not live on or near reservations. This difference makes cross-checking, interchanging, or comparing the two sets of data impossible. A glance at the basic head count for 1970 in a few states suggests the scope of the problem:

State	Census	BIA
Arizona	94,000	115,000
Oklahoma	97,000	81,000
Washington	31,000	16,000
California	88,000	38,000
North Carolina	44,000	5,000
Minnesota	22,000	11,000
25 nonreservation states	105,000	0

Since each source provides information unavailable elsewhere, it is necessary to use both, whatever problems of confusion and apparent inconsistency this may entail. Though the subsets are far from exact, the census classifications for rural Indians occasionally may be used in approximating conditions among Indians on or near reservations.

2. Based on census samples and does not match totals reported earlier.

Chapter 2

1. Alan L. Sorkin, *American Indians and Federal Aid* (Washington, D.C.: The Brookings Institution, 1971), p. 68.
2. U.S. Congress, House, *Department of the Interior and Related Agencies for 1975,* pt. 4, *Hearings* before a subcommittee of the Committee on Appropriations, 93rd Cong., 2d sess., (Washington, D.C.: Government Printing Office, 1973), pp. 244–45.
3. Sorkin, *American Indians,* p. 77.
4. Ibid., p. 95.

Chapter 3

1. *U.S. Department of Health, Education, and Welfare, Office for Civil Rights, Racial and Ethnic Enrollment Data from Institutions of Higher Learning, Fall 1970* (Washington, D.C.: Government Printing Office, 1972), pp. 116, 177, 185, 190, and 200.
2. U.S. Congress, House, *Department of the Interior and Related Agencies Appropriations for 1974,* pt. 4, *Hearings* before a subcommittee of the Committee on Appropriations, 93d Cong., 1st sess. (Washington, D.C.: Government Printing Office, 1973), p. 664.
3. James S. Coleman et al., *Equality of Educational Opportunity* (Washington, D.C.: Government Printing Office, 1966), pp. 20, 274–75.
4. Clennon E. Sockley, director of BIA education programs, letter to the author, September 16, 1974.
5. Daniel M. Rosenfelt, "The Renaissance of Indian Education," *Inequality in Education,* November 1973, pp. 13–21.
6. U.S. Congress, House, *Department of the Interior and Related Agencies Appropriations for 1975,* pt. 5, Duane Birrdbear, *Hearings* before a subcommittee of the Committee on Appropriations, 93d Cong., 2d sess. (Washington D.C.: Government Printing Office, 1974), p. 242.
7. Ibid., p. 228.

Chapter 4

1. U.S. Congress, *House, Department of the Interior and Related Agencies Appropriations for 1974,* pt. 4, *Hearings* before a subcommittee of the Committee on Appropriations, 93d Cong., 1st sess. (Washington, D.C.: Government Printing Office, 1973), pp. 40 and 91.

Chapter 5

1. Alan L. Sorkin, *American Indians and Federal Aid* (Washington, D.C.: The Brookings Institution, 1971), p. 1.
2. U.S. Congress, House, *Department of the Interior and Related Agencies Appropriations for 1975,* pt. 1, *Hearings* before a subcommittee of the Committee on Appropriations, 93d. Cong., 2d sess. (Washington, D.C.: Government Printing Office, 1974), p. 237.

3. U.S. Bureau of the Census, *1970 Census of the Population, American Indians,* PC(2)1F, (June 1973), Table 10, p. 129.

4. U.S. Congress, House, *Department of the Interior and Related Agencies Appropriation for 1973,* pt. 2, *Hearings* before a subcommittee of the Committee on Appropriations, 92d Cong., 2d sess. (Washington, D.C.: Government Printing Office, 1972), p. 127.

Library of Congress Cataloging in Publication Data

Lurie, Nancy O.
Indian policy: Federal programs for native
Americans.

(Policy studies in employment and welfare; no. 26)
Includes bibliographical references.
1. Indians of North America—Economic conditions.
2. Indians of North America—Social conditions.
3. Indians of North America—Government relations—
1934—   I. Johnson, William B., 1943—   joint
author.   II. Title.
E98.E2L84   301.451   75-11554
ISBN 0-8018-1739-0
ISBN 0-8018-1740-4 pbk.

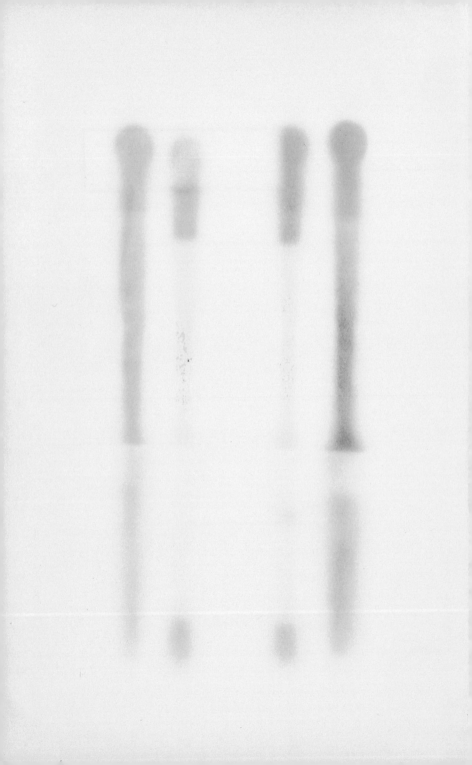